A HISTORY OF THE POPES

VOLUME II: EARLY MIDDLE AGES TO THE PROTESTANT REFORMATION

D1808550

Introduction 4

Saeculum Obscurum, Part I: Sergius III to Stephen VII (904–931)..9

Saeculum Obscurum, Part II: John XI to John XII (931–964)...........13

The End of the Early Middle Ages: Leo VIII to Gregory V (964–1012) 17

The Tusculan Papacy: Benedict VIII to Benedict IX (1012–1048).22

The German Popes and the Reformer Popes: Damasus II to Alexander II (1048–1073)..26

The Monarchical Papacy and the First Crusade: St. Gregory VII to Bl. Urban II (1073–1099)...30

The End of the Investiture Controversy: Paschal II to Honorius II (1099–1030) 34

Roman Intrigue, the Second Crusade, and the Rise of Frederick Barbarossa: Innocent II to Adrian IV (1130–1159) 39

Conflict between Barbarossa and the Papacy and the Third Crusade: Alexander III to Celestine III (1159–1198).........43

Frederick II and the Fourth and Fifth Crusades: Innocent III to Gregory IX (1198–1241)..47

The End of the Hohenstaufen Dynasty: Celestine IV to Clement IV (1241–1268) 52

The Angevin Rule of Sicily and Its Decline: Bl. Gregory X to Nicholas IV (1272–1292)...56

King Philip IV of France and the Colonna Family: St. Celestine V to Bl. Benedict XI (1294–1304)..................................62

The Avignon Papacy: Clement V to Gregory XI (1305–1378)..........66

The Great Western Schism: Urban VI to Gregory XII (1378–1415)72

The Transition into the Renaissance: Martin V to Callixtus III (1417–1458) 76

The Middle of the Renaissance Papacy: Pius II to Sixtus IV (1458–1484) 80

The Beginning of the Protestant Reformation: Innocent VIII to Leo X (1484–1521)...84

Conclusion: Recapitulation and a Look Ahead 89

Introduction

The office of bishop of Rome, is one of the most powerful positions in the world. As an ancient institution stretching back for centuries, the papacy has a history that is marked by archaic and modern customs alike. The history of the men who have held this position is fraught with villainous and heroic actions that have left a profound impact on the development of civilization as we know it, both in the West and East. The popes led the early Church through persecution, acquired temporal power through the actions of Constantine, oversaw the universal Church in the early middle ages, were steeped in various scandals in the late middle ages, saw their secular power stripped in the modern period, and were instrumental in the rise and fall of various kingdoms and nations.

Adding to the mystique of the papacy is the claim that the pope has a special charism called infallibility, meaning that when he teaches in his office as the successor of Peter on matters of faith or morals, he cannot err. How can such a claim be made seriously, especially in today's world where scientific rationalism pervades the mentality of modern men and women? The answer to this question goes back to Scripture. The Catholic Church interpreted several Scripture passages in the Gospel, in particular Matthew 16:16-19, as containing in seed form the doctrine of papal infallibility. At the First Vatican Council the bishops declared, "For the Holy Spirit was not promised to the successors of Peter that they might disclose a new doctrine by his revelation, but rather that, with his assistance, they might reverently guard and faithfully explain the revelation or deposit of faith that was handed down through the apostles" (Denzinger, §3070).

Jesus declared to Peter, "[Y]ou are Peter, and upon this rock I will build my church, and the gates of the netherworld shall not prevail against it. I will give you the keys to the kingdom of heaven. Whatever you bind on earth shall be bound in heaven; and whatever you loose on earth shall be loosed in heaven" (Matthew 16:18–19, New American Bible, Revised Edition). At the same time, Peter denied Jesus three times (Matthew 26:69–75). How was Peter, a weak man, ever to hope to have the strength to lead Jesus' followers? How can this prophecy be applicable to all of the successors of Peter throughout history when there were some popes who were downright evil? Cardinal Ratzinger, who later became Pope Benedict XVI, offered the following explanation: "The men in question are so glaringly, so blatantly unequal to this function that the very empowerment of man to be the rock makes evident how little it is they who sustain the Church but God alone who does so, who does so more in spite of men than through them" (Ratzinger, 73). God uses weak instruments to accomplish his tasks; this is the best answer there is. Taken as a whole, the history of the popes is more sad and tragic than it is glorious. Seen from the perspective of the Catholic Church's endurance, regardless of the frightening waves that have pounded its bark, it is truly miraculous that the papacy has withstood the test of time and has lasted for millennia, whereas other nations, kingdoms, and institutions inevitably erode with time.

This present volume begins with a historical sketch of Peter and the role he played in the early Church. It is apparent from the New Testament that Peter enjoyed some kind of primacy over the other apostles and that Jesus' intention was not to set up Peter as a rock, since Peter himself could never endure for generations, but as an institution with power and authority, hence the ability to bind and to loose (Matthew 16:19). Of course, this same power was given to the rest of the apostles as well (Matthew 18:18), but it was first promised to Peter, to whom Jesus gave the charge of strengthening his brothers (Luke 22:32).

This work, which is conceived as a three volume history of the popes, is not intended to be a theological treatise on papal primacy or infallibility, nor is it a look at the lives of the popes as though it were a collection of miniature biographical sketches; instead, it is intended to be a history of the popes. It is concerned with the pontificates of the individual popes and how their pontificates shaped the papacy, the Catholic Church and the world. For this purpose, each chapter is divided into a historical epoch, a period of history spanning from a decade to a century. Within these spaces of time, the most significant actions of the popes will be described and their impact assessed.

I follow Richard McBrien's dates for the beginnings of each pontificate, which differs slightly from the official dates. The official dates in the Vatican lists do not consider the theological question of whether an elected pope who was not a consecrated bishop, can be considered pope, since by definition the pope is the bishop of Rome. The official lists seem to ignore this fact, whereas McBrien carefully takes into consideration the date of a papal candidate's episcopal ordination.

Because this work is going to cover two millennia of history, I will divide it into three volumes. The first volume will cover roughly the first nine hundred years of papal history up to the pontificate of Leo V. The second volume will cover the pontificates from the infamous Sergius III to Leo X. Finally, the third volume will cover the popes of the late renaissance period to the modern era, which spans from the pontificate of Adrian VI to that of Francis. The rationale for this division is that more is known about recent popes than the early popes, so it makes sense to devote one volume to the popes in the first nine hundred years. The division between the second and third volumes coincides with the dawn of the Protestant Reformation. Leo X was pope during 1517, when Martin Luther nailed his *Ninety-five Theses* on the doors of the church at Wittenberg, Germany. The Catholic Church's response to Protestantism and their own Counter Reformation are a major theme of the third volume.

Despite the vast scope of this project, the relatively small size of the three volumes, a little over sixty thousand words in total, means that on average, I can only devote thirty words per year of history. For this reason, I will have to paint with rather broad strokes in such a way as to give a complete picture without dwelling on too many particular details.

Hopefully, the reader will get a sense of the remarkable image of the history of the popes with all of its shade and light, scandals and wonders, failures and achievements.

Saeculum Obscurum, Part I:
Sergius III to Stephen VII (904–931)

This era in papal history, sometimes referred to as *saeculum obscurum*, is also known by another vulgar phrase, "pornocracy," or rule of the prostitutes. It is certainly one of the low points in the Catholic Church's history and demonstrates the level of debasement some successors of St. Peter stooped, but it also demonstrates that it is only through the grace of God that the Catholic Church has endured, despite some of its immoral pontiffs.

At the end of 903 in Rome, the papacy was in turmoil. Coveting the papacy, Sergius marched on Rome and had both the antipope Christopher and Leo V strangled to death in prison. He then succeeded Leo V on January 29, 904, and took the name Sergius III. He nullified Formosus's acts and upheld the proceedings of the Cadaver Synod. A man with strong ties among the nobles, Sergius was a friend of Theophylact, the commander of one of the militias in the region. Sergius is said to have fathered a son, with Marozia the fifteen-year-old daughter of Theodora and Theophylact, who later became Pope John XI. In fact, several popes were direct descendants of Marozia.

Sticking his nose in the affairs of the East and completely disregarding Byzantine canon law, Sergius approved emperor

Leo IV's marriage and deposed the patriarch of Constantinople who had stood in the way. Sergius restored the Lateran Basilica after it had been damaged during the Cadaver Synod, a sign to pro-Formosans that God was angered by the spectacle. Unlike many of his predecessors, Sergius did not have many enemies with power and had a relatively long papacy; he died on April 14, 911.

Anastasius III succeeded Sergius circa June 911. Little is known of Anastasius's pontificate, which was dominated by the Theophylact family. The restored patriarch of Constantinople, Nicholas, whom Sergius had deposed for standing in the way of Leo's marriage, wrote a letter to Anastasius complaining of Sergius's deeds. Apparently Anastasius's reply had not make Nicholas happy since Nicholas struck Anastasius's name off of the list of people to be prayed for at Mass. Anastasius died circa August 913.

Lando succeeded Anastasius III circa August 913. Historians believe that he had the support of the Theophylact family. He is said to have made a donation in honor of his father, but other than this, very little is known of his pontificate. Lando died circa March 914.

John X succeeded Lando in March 914. He had been the bishop of Ravenna before his election. The Theophylact family ensured John's election since he was known as a skilled leader, something the Romans desperately needed due to the Saracens constantly raiding Italy. John X brought together a coalition of armies under various Italian princes and also accosted Constantine VII to send a naval fleet to assist in the effort to hold back the Saracen invaders. The Saracens were defeated in 915, and Berengar was subsequently crowned emperor in St. Peters.

In ecclesiastical matters, John was an astute and pious leader. He sought to restore the unity between East and West and was able to patch up their relationship in 923. He was insistent, however, on replacing the Slavonic liturgy with the Roman liturgy in Dalmatia, but was not successful. Closer to home, John was forced to ordain the five-year-old son of Count Herbert, the archbishop of Rheims, because of political threats. John was a big supporter of monasticism, especially the form of monasticism found in the new abbey of Cluny.

John's pontificate came to a tragic end when he attempted to distance himself from the Roman nobles. When Theophylact and Berengar died, John made a pact with Hugh of Provence, the new king of Italy. Unhappy with this arrangement, Marozia and her husband Guido, the marquis of Tuscany, plotted John X's overthrow. They put the pope's brother, Peter, to death in the Lateran in front of the pope, deposed the pope in May 928, and put him in a dungeon, where he died several months later by suffocation under the orders of Marozia in 929.

Leo VI, an elderly priest when elected to the papacy, succeeded John X in May 928 even though John X was still alive in prison. The only surviving text from Leo's pontificate is a letter he wrote to the bishops of Dalmatia and Croatia in which he instructed them to listen to the archbishop he had placed over them. Leo died in December 928.

Stephen VII succeeded Leo VI in December 928. He also had been elected while John X was still alive. Like Leo VI, he served as a place-holder for the candidate of the Theophylact family, since Marozia wanted her son to be pope. Stephen died in February 931. With the death of Stephen, the Theophylact family could finally install one of their own on the Chair of Peter, thus extending their power and authority in Rome and Italy.

Saeculum Obscurum, Part II:
John XI to John XII (931–964)

John XI, the illegitimate son of Pope Sergius III and Marozia, succeeded Stephen VII in March 931, while he was in his early twenties. He ensured the abbey of Cluny that the Holy See would offer them protection. He also approved the appointment of a sixteen-year-old as the patriarch of Constantinople and sent two bishops to consecrate him. Later, when Guido had died, Marozia decided to marry Hugh of Provence, the king of Italy. John officiated at the wedding, even though the wedding was not considered canonical since Hugh was Marozia's brother-in-law. After being insulted by Hugh at the wedding feast, Alberic II, Marozia's son by her first marriage—the pope's half-brother—incited a revolt. Alberic had Marozia and John arrested. While Marozia apparently died in prison,since nothing else is known of her, John was released and put under house arrest. John XI died in December 935, when he was still in his twenties.

Leo VII succeeded John XI on January 3, 936. Alberic heavily influenced the election in Leo's favor. Most likely a Benedictine himself, Leo sought to revive monasticism and brought Odo of Cluny to Rome to reform the religious houses in Rome. He died on July 13, 939.

Stephen VIII succeeded Leo VII on July 14, 939. Alberic also orchestrated this election so that it would be in Stephen's favor. Stephen supported Louis IV as king of France. Toward the end of Stephen's papacy, Alberic put the pope in prison and mutilated him, possibly as a punishment for conspiring against him. Stephen died of his wounds in October 942.

Marinus II succeeded Stephen VIII on October 30, 942. Like Leo VII and Stephen VIII, Marinus owed his pontificate to Alberic and was essentially powerless except in ecclesiastical matters. He arbitrated in a dispute between the bishop of Capua and the abbey of Monte Casino, ruling in favor of the latter. Marinus II died in May 946.

Agapitus II succeeded Marinus II on May 10, 946. Like his three immediate predecessors, he became pope through the scheming of Alberic. Agapitus supported the Cluny monastic reform and sought to increase the discipline of the monks in Rome. The pope also was politically active. He ratified a synod where King Otto I of Germany and King Louis IV of France were present and he gave his support to Otto. When Alberic was on his death bed, he had forced Agapitus and all the Roman clergy to take an oath that the next pope would be Octavian, Alberic's son. Agapitus died in December of 955.

John XII succeeded Agapitus II on December 16, 955. Known as Octavian before becoming pope, John XII was the son of Alberic II and the grandson of Marozia—making him the great-grandson of Theophylact and Theodora, and the nephew of John XI. John was the youngest man to become pope, having been elected at the age of eighteen, and his pontificate is one of the most scandalous in history. He was accused of turning the Lateran into a brothel and of committing fornication and adultery. It has also been said that John invoked the names of pagan gods while playing dice, toasted to the devil, blinded his confessor, and committed arson. While these accusations came from Liudprand of Cremona, a bitter enemy of John XII, there were other contemporaries of John XII who corroborated Liudprand's descriptions of John's character.

In 962 John established the Holy Roman Empire by crowning Otto I emperor. John and Otto, however, had a falling out when Otto granted the Church the Ottonian Privilege, an arrangement in which the donations of Pepin and Charlemagne were recognized and in which the Papal States were aggrandized through the annexation of other territories. John had not liked the part of the arrangement in which the popes had to recognize the emperor as the supreme ruler of the Papal States, and decided to conspire against Otto with the help of Berengar II, the king of Italy. When word got to Otto, he marched to Italy and John fled. Otto presided over a synod in which John XII had been accused of immorality and in which he was deposed after refusing to come to the synod after being summoned three times. Otto then suggested that Leo, a layman, become pope in John's stead. John XII died at the age of twenty-eight after suffering a stroke while he was in bed with a married woman on May 14, 964.

The end of John XII's papacy marked the end of *saeculum obscurum*, but it did not mark the last time a member of the Theophylact family would be elected pope. In fact, the last Theophylact family member to become pope—who was incidentally named Theophylact— was Benedict IX, who was pope on three separate occasions spanning from 1032 to 1048.

The End of the Early Middle Ages:
Leo VIII to Gregory V (964–1012)

The annals of the next period of papal history, which saw the end of the Early Middle Ages, is filled with more immoral popes, but is also the time when the power of the Theophylact family began to wane. Leo VIII technically became antipope on December 6, 963, at the behest of Otto after the emperor had John XII deposed, and his canonical papacy did not begin until the end of Benedict V's pontificate. The election of Leo VIII to the papacy was rather dubious since John XII was still alive, but the official list of popes at the Vatican accepts the overlapping papacies of John XII and Leo VIII. Leo had been a layman who was rushed through minor and major orders before he was consecrated as bishop of Rome. Leo was not popular with the common people, who had asked Otto to appoint Benedict V pope in John's place. Otto, having appointed Leo, refused. Leo died on March 1, 965.

Benedict V was elected pope after the death of John XII by the Roman populace, who did not accept the papacy of Leo VIII; this was the first time in many years that a pope had not been put on the Chair of Peter through the scheming of one of the Theophylact family members. He was pope from May 22 to June 23, 964, for only one month. During this time, Otto besieged Rome until the people handed Benedict over to the emperor. After condemning and deposing Benedict V to the rank of deacon, Leo VIII exiled him to Hamburg and became the canonical bishop of Rome.

John XIII became pope on October 1, 965, after the death of Leo VIII. John was essentially the pawn of Otto I, who ensured that John was elected. Otto II, Otto's twelve-year-old son, was crowned as co-emperor by John XIII in 967. When he was seventeen, Otto II married the niece of John I, the Byzantine emperor, in a ceremony presided over by John XIII. It was hoped that relations between the East and the West would have been improved through this marriage, but it did not help to hold back the widening fissure between the two realms. John XIII died on September 6, 972.

Benedict VI succeeded John XIII on January 19, 973. The powerful Crescentii family favored Cardinal Franco Ferrucci, one of their own, as the next pope after John XIII died. When Benedict VI became pope instead, the Crescentii family plotted Benedict's overthrow, imprisoned him in one of their castles, and had Franco Ferruci ordained as bishop of Rome, who took the name Boniface VII. When Otto II heard of the state of affairs and sent a delegation to Rome to investigate, antipope Boniface gave orders to a priest to murder the pope. Benedict VI was strangled to death in June 974.

Benedict VII succeeded Benedict VI in October 974. The new pope immediately excommunicated antipope Boniface VII, who then conspired against Benedict. After escaping a plot by Boniface, Benedict turned his attention to other ecclesiastical affairs. He was primarily interested in his role as spiritual leader and not in politics, although he was essentially Otto II's puppet in various political affairs. Benedict promoted monasticism and held a synod in 981 in which he condemned simony. After nearly nine years in office, Benedict died on July 10, 983.

John XIV succeeded Benedict VII in December 983. He did not keep his birth name because it was Peter and he did not want to be known as Peter II. The appointee of Otto II, John XIV had no allies other than the emperor. When Otto II died shortly after John became pope, John was defenseless. Antipope Boniface VII came to Rome and had John arrested, deposed, and imprisoned in one of the Crescentii strongholds where he died a few months later on August 20, 984, either through starvation or poisoning.

John XV succeeded John XIV in August 985, nearly a year after John XIV's reign since Boniface VII had control, even though he was not the legitimate pope. When Boniface VII died in July 985, the people of Rome dragged his naked body through the streets and referred to him as Malefatius or "evildoer" instead of Bonifatius which means "doer of good." It was not until 1904 that Boniface VII was considered an antipope. John XV was the first pope to canonize a saint, St. Ulric. John's papacy was marked by a strong attention to political affairs. His avarice, politicking, and his desire to please the aristocracy, alienated him from his clergy. John XV died of a fever in March 996.

Gregory V succeeded John XV on May 3, 996 when he was only twenty-four years old. Born Bruno of Carinthia, upon his election the new pope chose to be called Gregory after Gregory the Great. Although there were other popes of Germanic background, Gregory V is considered to have been the first German pope. He crowned Otto III as emperor on May 21, 996. The Romans were not pleased with the foreign pope and when the emperor left Rome to go back to Germany, the Romans – under the Crescentii family – drove out Gregory, who subsequently excommunicated the head of the Crescentii family. Shortly after in 997, the Crescentii family declared the archbishop of Piacenza to be Pope John XVI. When Gregory came back to Rome with the emperor, antipope John was excommunicated and imprisoned, and Crescentius, the head of the Crescentii family, was beheaded. Gregory V died of malaria on February 18, 999.

Sylvester II, the first French pope, succeeded Gregory V on April 2, 999. Born Gerbert d'Aurillac, Sylvester was extremely well-educated in liberal arts and mathematics. He was one of the most renowned mathematicians, educators, and scientists of his generation. In fact, it was Sylvester who introduced the decimal system and Arabic numerals to Europe. He also was responsible for reintroducing both the abacus and the armillary sphere to Western Europe. In addition to his work in science and mathematics, Sylvester introduced Aristotle to the West. After he had been elected pope, Sylvester sought to reform the Church by banning simony and nepotism and by seeking to purge abbot elections in monasteries of intrigue and force. Although Gerbert had chosen the name Sylvester to indicate his cooperation with the emperor Otto III, to be modeled after the cooperation of Sylvester and Constantine, Sylvester asserted his papal prerogatives once he was pope. When Otto III died, John Crescentii allowed the pope to stay in Rome provided that he limit his activity to the spiritual realm. Sylvester died on May 12, 1003.

John XVII, most likely a member of the Crescentii family, succeeded Sylvester II on May 16, 1003. He had been married before he was pope and had three sons. John died on November 6, 1003, after a brief pontificate of six months. John XVIII succeeded John XVII on December 25, 1003. Not an especially powerful pope on account of being under the sway of the Crescentii family, John primarily concerned himself with ecclesiastical affairs. He eventually abdicated in July 1009.

Sergius IV succeeded John XVIII on July 31, 1009. Since his birth name was Peter, he changed his name to Sergius upon his election. His election was the result of the influence of the Crescentii family. Some speculate that Sergius and John II Crescentius were both murdered since they disappeared within a week of each other. Sergius's papacy ended on May 12, 1012. With the deaths of Sergius IV and John II Crescentius came the end of the dominance of the Crescentii family.

The Tusculan Papacy:
Benedict VIII to Benedict IX (1012–1048)

The Theophylact family rose again in power in 1012 against their rivals, the Crescentii family. Benedict VIII—the great-great-grandson of Theophylact, the great-grandson of Marozia, and the nephew of Pope John XII—succeeded Sergius IV on May 18, 1012. Only a layman when elected pope, Benedict VIIIwhose birth name was Theophylact like his ancestor, was a political pope. Benedict used military force to oppose the Crescentii family and to secure his position on the Chair of Peter, after which he established relations with Henry II, the German emperor. In another military exploit, Benedict personally led a naval fleet against Saracen invaders. In addition to this he sought the aid of Henry II in response to the Byzantine threat. A synod was held in Pavia in which it was established that those who had been ordained to the order of subdeacon could no longer get married. After a powerful military and political career, Benedict died on April 9, 1024.

John XIX succeeded Benedict VIII, his brother, on April 19, 1024. Born Romanus, John obtained the papacy on account of the power of the Tusculan family, a new branch of the Theophylact family. He had also been a layman before he was selected for the papacy and was rushed through holy orders. Scandalized, the Roman populace did not hold John in high regard. Although John crowned Conrad II emperor in 1027, Conrad ungratefully refused to renew the privileges normally granted to the Holy See by the emperors. John XIX died on October 20, 1032.

Benedict IX, the son of Alberic III, succeeded John XIX on October 21, 1032. Like both of his uncles, Benedict VIII and John XIX, Benedict IX had been a layman before he became pope and was rushed through holy orders. He was the only pope to have ever held the papacy for three separate periods. Born Theophylact, Benedict IX was ushered into the papacy through the bribery of his powerful family. As such, it was no surprise that he kept his own family in mind when making decisions. Nevertheless, Benedict was ecclesiastically active and doctrinally orthodox. He placed the abbey of Monte Cassino under the aegis of the Holy See in 1038. Unhappy with young Benedict—who was twenty when he became pope—and with the dominance of the Tusculan family, the Romans revolted and Benedict had to flee Rome in 1044. Although Benedict had never been officially deposed, the Crescentii family set up Sylvester III as pope in 1045. Benedict excommunicated Sylvester and was able to drive him out of Rome, but he abdicated shortly thereafter in favor of Gregory VI—Benedict may have sold his office to Gregory.

Although the legitimacy of Sylvester III's pontificate was questionable, he is still on official Vatican lists of popes. He was put in power by the Crescentii family on January 20, 1045, only to be driven out of Rome by Benedict IX two months later.

Gregory VI became pope on May 5, 1045, but was accused of simony and deposed for accepting the papacy in exchange for a large sum of money he had given to Benedict IX, his godson. Moreover, canon law ruled against Benedict IX choosing his own successor. Therefore, when the German ruler Henry III came to Rome in the fall of 1046 hoping to be crowned emperor by the pope, he was dismayed to find three possible candidates: Benedict IX, Sylvester III, and Gregory VI. All three candidates were deposed, and Suidger of Bamberg became pope, taking the name of Clement II. Gregory was deposed on December 20, 1046.

Clement II succeeded Gregory VI on December 25, 1046. The new pope immediately held a synod in which simony was condemned. Henry's choice of a pope suited the Germans well; in fact, he was one of four German popes installed by Henry III. Clement crowned Henry as Holy Roman Emperor, but on his way back to Rome, Clement suddenly died on October 9, 1047. It was rumored that Clement had been poisoned. A toxicological examination in 1942 indicated that Clement died of poisoning by lead sugar, but it is not known whether he was murdered by Benedict IX or used the lead sugar for medicine.

Benedict IX became pope for an unprecedented third time on November 8, 1047, but was forced to abdicate by an imperial decree on July 16, 1048. Benedict went back to his homeland where he licked his wounds and continued to delude himself with visions of grandeur by considering himself to be the true pope. When he was asked to appear before a synod in 1049 to face the charge of simony and refused to come, Benedict was excommunicated. He died in late 1055 or early 1056. With the end of Benedict IX's pontificate, the Tusculan papacy had come to an end.

The German Popes and the Reformer Popes: Damasus II to Alexander II (1048–1073)

Damasus II succeeded Benedict IX on July 17, 1048. When Henry III heard that Clement II had died, he nominated Poppo, the bishop of Brixen. However, when Poppo attempted to enter Rome, the Tusculan family refused to allow him to enter. Benedict IX still wanted to be pope and had made his way back to Rome. Poppo reported back to Henry, who then threatened the count that he would come down to Rome in person and install a new pope. When the count relented, Benedict was removed from Rome and Poppo was consecrated Damasus II. His was a short-lived pontificate however; Damasus died on August 9, 1048.

St. Leo IX succeeded Damasus II on February 12, 1049. Although he had been nominated by Henry III, Leo sought the approval of the clergy and people of Rome. The Roman people joyfully accepted him when he came to Rome in modest pilgrim attire. He called a synod that condemned simony and put together a cabinet of sorts. Two of the people in the pope's inner circle were Hildebrand, who later became Pope Gregory VII, and Humbert of Moyenmoutier. Leo travelled extensively throughout Europe during his pontificate. Toward the end of his reign however, Leo met several setbacks. A military expedition he had inaugurated against the Normans ended in disaster, and he was captured by the enemy and held for almost a year. In 1053 Michael Cerularius, the patriarch of Constantinople, became more belligerent in his anti-Latin stances. A Latin delegation headed by Humbert went to Constantinople in 1054. Since neither side was willing to budge, the tenuous unity between East and West rapidly dissolved on July 16, 1054, when Humbert placed a papal document on the altar of Hagia Sophia excommunicating the patriarch of Constantinople. Both sides ended up excommunicating each other and the schism still exists today. While Leo died before the schism occurred, the delegation was acting in his name. Leo died on April 19, 1054, and his feast day is celebrated on April 19.

Victor II succeeded Leo IX on April 13, 1055. The last of the four German popes nominated by Henry III, Victor held a synod condemning simony and clerical marriage. He swiftly excommunicated a number of bishops. When Henry III died in 1056, Victor went to Aachen, where he crowned the five-year-old Henry IV as king and proclaimed Henry's mother, Agnes, his regent. Victor died on July 28, 1057.

Stephen IX succeeded Victor II on August 2, 1057. Born Frederick, Stephen had been the abbot of Monte Cassino when he was elected pope. He chose the name of Stephen since

August 2 was Stephen I's feast day. Stephen attempted to implement reform in Monte Cassino, where he sought to go back to the original rule of poverty rather than opulence, and he supported clerical celibacy. Hildebrand and Humbert were some of Stephen's closest advisors. Stephen's brief pontificate ended abruptly before he was finished with his reform efforts; he died on March 29, 1058.

Nicholas II succeeded Stephen IX on January 24, 1059. When Stephen IX was still pope, he had ordered the cardinals that if he were to die before Hildebrand returned from a mission, that they were to wait for Hildebrand's return before commencing the papal election. An impatient faction in Rome elected John, the bishop of Velletri—who took the name of Benedict X—without the full support of all the cardinals. The rest of the cardinals, with the support of Hildebrand, elected Gerard, the bishop of Florence, who took the name of Nicholas II. Benedict X fled Rome, and Nicholas excommunicated and deposed him. Unlike his predecessors, Nicholas allied himself with the Normans instead of fighting them. Early during Nicholas's pontificate in 1059, a synod was held in which the bishops changed the way papal elections were determined. Previously, papal elections had been determined or approved by political leaders, but it was now decided that cardinal-bishops would hold the papal elections and that the pope would be selected from among the cardinals. This was a watershed decision in papal history which truly changed the course of history. Nicholas died on July 27, 1061.

Alexander II succeeded Nicholas II on September 30, 1061. Although the Lateran synod in 1059 held that papal elections would now be determined by cardinal bishops, the German imperial court nominated its own pope, Honorius II, who overpowered Alexander's forces and had himself installed as pope in Rome. When the duke of Lorraine arrived in Rome, he ruled that both claimants to the papacy should return to their dioceses until the court settled the matter. Eventually, the court determined that Alexander was the rightfully elected pope.

In certain respects, some of the pontifical acts of Alexander II prefigured the Crusades. He granted indulgences to Norman soldiers in Sicily and French knights in Spain, who were fighting against the Muslims. At the same time, he sought to defend the Jews from abuse by the Christian soldiers involved in these campaigns. Alexander was a reformer at heart, attacking simony, taking a strong stance against divorce and remarriage, prohibiting lay investiture, and encouraging clergy in cathedrals to live a common life. The pope also reached out to the East by sending a delegation to the Byzantine emperor, but it produced no fruit.

The church and state clashed in the persons of Alexander II and Henry IV in 1071. Henry wanted to install someone as archbishop of Milan, whereas Alexander had another candidate in mind. Seeing that Henry was intransigent, Alexander excommunicated five of Henry's advisors for simony. This struggle between church and state continued under the pontificate of Alexander's successor, St. Gregory VII, after Alexander's death on April 21, 1073.

The Monarchical Papacy and the First Crusade: St. Gregory VII to Bl. Urban II (1073–1099)

St. Gregory VII succeeded Alexander II on June 30, 1073. His pontificate is widely regarded as one of the most significant in papal history. Born Hildebrand, Gregory already had a lot of ecclesiastical experience under his belt when he was elected, having worked with Gregory VI, Leo IX, Nicholas II, and Alexander II. At the time of his election, Gregory had been an archdeacon. In contrast to his immediate predecessors, Gregory was selected as pope by popular acclaim of the Romans and their wish was confirmed by the cardinals. Like his predecessors, Gregory was a reformer pope. He denounced simony, enforced the rule of celibacy for priests and bishops, and virtually rewrote the prerogatives of the papacy through his *Dictatus papae* the "Pronouncements of the Pope," which claimed a far-reaching power for the papacy. He claimed that only the pope had the right to appoint or depose bishops, or to transfer them to other sees.

Ambitious, Gregory had lofty goals for the Church. He wanted to rescue the Holy Sepulchre from Muslim control and wanted to reconcile the East and West, but the Investiture Controversy in Europe demanded his attention throughout his pontificate.

Gregory's strong stance in regard to the issue of investiture, i.e. the installment of laymen as clerics by political figures, brought him in direct conflict with Henry IV. The German emperor had appointed his own candidates as bishops and abbots in various parts of Germany and Italy. When Gregory reproached Henry, Henry called a synod and had Gregory deposed. From a political standpoint, Gregory's reply was brilliant: he excommunicated Henry, declared that his imperial prerogatives were suspended, and released his subjects from owing allegiance to him. With his political power in jeopardy, Henry walked through the snow in penitential garb in January 1077 to plead forgiveness from Gregory. The pope gave the emperor absolution, but three years later another dispute erupted between the two men. The German princes who had seen the excommunication of Henry as an opportunity to aggrandize their power, had set up a rival king, Rudolf of Swabia. After a long time of embracing a policy of neutrality, Gregory gave his support to Rudolf and excommunicated Henry. This time however, the king claimed that Gregory had exceeded his bounds. After Henry called another synod, Gregory was yet again deposed. The pope's decision was not popular with the Roman people and the clergy: he lost the support of thirteen cardinals. Henry marched on Rome and recognized the enthronement of

Clement III, an antipope elected by the Roman clergy and laity in the place of Gregory. Robert Guiscard, the duke of Apulia, rescued the pope with his troops and Henry and Clement both fled. However, the violence of Robert's troops outraged the Romans who turned on Gregory. The pope left Rome and, after going to Monte Cassino and Salerno, died on May 25, 1085. Gregory's feast day is celebrated on May 25.

Bl. Victor III succeeded St. Gregory VII on May 9, 1087. Born Daufer, Victor entered the religious life at a young age and chose the name Desiderius when he entered the abbey of Monte Cassino. After he became abbot, Desiderius became a cardinal under Nicholas II. At first, Victor resisted since he knew that he was getting old—he supported Cardinal Oddone di Châtillon, who took the name Urban II after he succeeded Victor—but eventually he accepted his election. He travelled back and forth between Rome and Monte Cassino and although he upheld Gregory VII's stance on lay investiture, Victor's health declined rapidly and he died on September 16, 1087, before he could implement major reforms. Victor's feast day is celebrated on September 16.

Bl. Urban II succeeded Victor III on March 12, 1088. Urban is best known for launching the First Crusade and for establishing the Roman Curia. He had been the former abbot of Cluny in Burgundy and was the cardinal-bishop of Ostia when he was elected to the papacy. From the outset of his election, Urban had to worry about Clement III, the antipope. In fact, the papal election in which it was determined that Urban would be Victor's successor occurred outside of Rome since Clement III had control of the city. Perhaps he chose Urban as his papal name since the original Urban also had a rival to the papacy, antipope Hippolytus. Henry IV was still upset at Gregory's insistence that the emperor had no power to choose his own candidates to become bishops and abbots, so he forced Urban out of Rome and let Clement III take up his residence in the Eternal City. Eventually in 1093, Urban was able to make it back to Rome after Henry's son, Conrad, gave his support to the pope.

On a cold day in late November 1095, Pope Urban gave a rousing speech at the Council of Clermont in which he urged Christians to liberate Christian churches in the Holy Lands from Muslim rule. The people in reply proclaimed, *"Deus vult!"* which means "God wills it!" Urban's sermon moved the people so deeply that it ended internecine skirmishes, galvanized Europe, and effectively extended a spiritual olive branch to men of war. Urban promised that a great indulgence—a temporal remission of the punishment due to sin— would be available to any man who set out with pure intentions to conquer the Holy Land not for personal glory, but solely for the glory of God. From 1095 to 1099, for better or for worse, the First Crusade was fought with much vigor until Jerusalem was conquered by the Crusaders in 1099, two weeks after Urban had died on July 29, 1099. Urban's feast day is celebrated on July 29.

The End of the Investiture Controversy:
Paschal II to Honorius II (1099–1030)

Paschal II succeeded Urban II on August 14, 1099. His nearly two-decade long pontificate was unusually long for a medieval pope. Although he attempted to keep up the reform of his predecessors, he gave many concessions to Henry V, thus inadvertently decreasing the prestige of the papacy. Created a cardinal by Gregory VII, Paschal had to contend with four antipopes while he was pope, including Clement III, whom Paschal was eventually able to oust from Rome with help from the Normans. Henry V wanted to continue investing his own candidates as clergy and when Paschal refused, the two of them eventually arrived at a compromise. However, since the concordat was unpopular with the people of Rome, Henry put the pope and other Roman clergy, including the future pope Gelasius II, in prison where Paschal was forced to give way to more conciliations: Henry would be allowed to confirm papal candidates and invest them with the episcopal ring and crozier.

Although Paschal was under dire circumstances and forced to a compromise he would not have agreed to had he been in a more favorable environment, his acquiescence to Henry V created a firestorm of protest among the Hildebrandian reformers. Eventually, Paschal abrogated the agreement he made with Henry. In England, Paschal supported St. Anselm of

Canterbury in his struggle against lay investiture with Henry I. The French king was content with replacing his prerogative of investiture with an oath of allegiance from the newly ordained clergy. In the East, Paschal was unable to broker a peace with the Eastern emperor, Alexius I Comenus, who had reached out to him. Instead of being flexible and open to dialogue, Paschal insisted that the East recognize papal primacy as a prerequisite for reestablishing communion. As much as Alexius may have been willing to concede to this, Paschal knew that the patriarch of Constantinople would never agree to this condition. Paschal died on January 21, 1118.

Gelasius II succeeded Paschal II on March 10, 1118. Born Giovanni, Gelasius entered the monastery of Monte Cassino at an early age. He was chancellor of the Holy Roman Church for nearly three decades from 1089 to 1118 under Urban II and Paschal II, and was responsible for some of the major evolutionary changes in the papal administration. Shortly after he was elected pope, but before he was consecrated bishop or priest, Gelasius was imprisoned by an anti-Paschalian patrician family in Rome. Protesting the pope-elect's imprisonment, the aristocratic families secured Gelasius's release, but as soon as he was out of prison he fled with the cardinals to his homeland, Gaeta, a port city about seventy-five miles southeast of Rome, where he received his presbyteral and episcopal ordinations, since Henry V was marching toward Rome. Henry sent a message to Gelasius demanding that he come back to Rome so that the two could come to an agreement on the investiture issue, but when Gelasius refused, Henry installed an antipope who took the name of Gregory VIII. In reply, Gelasius excommunicated both Henry V and Gregory VIII. Upon his return to Rome, Gelasius found that it was under the control of Gregory VIII. He had to flee Rome once again and this time went to France where he died on January 28, 1119, at the abbey of Cluny.

When Gelasius died at Cluny, the cardinals who had accompanied him elected Guido, the archbishop of Vienne, as pope on February 2, 1119. The cardinals in Rome were notified of the election and ratified it. Immediately, the new pope, who took the name Callixtus II, had to deal with the investiture controversy. From the beginning, Callixtus carried out his reformist agenda with vigor and success. He reaffirmed his condemnation of lay investiture and excommunicated Henry V at a council in Rheims that was attended by Louis VI, the king of France. Callixtus was joyfully received at Rome, and after Gregory VIII was handed over to Callixtus, the pope gave him a rather lenient sentence, confining him to a monastery. In 1122, Henry V, under pressure from German princes to settle the matter of lay investiture, came to an agreement with Callixtus in a document known as the *Concordat of Worms*. According to the agreement, "the emperor renounced his putative right to invest bishops and abbots with ring and crozier (symbols of spiritual authority), and the free elections and consecrations of bishops and abbots were guaranteed. In return, the pope conceded to Henry the assurance that the elections of bishops and abbots in Germany would be held in his presence and that Henry would invest those elected with the symbol of temporal authority (the scepter)" (McBrien, 195). The *Concordat of Worms* was approved ecclesiastically at the First Lateran Council in 1123; the lay investiture controversy had finally ended. Callixtus died on December 13, 1124.

Honorius II succeeded Callixtus II on December 21, 1124. Born Lamberto, Honorius had played a role in drafting the *Concordat of Worms*. His election was quite dramatic. Rome was split into two powerful families: the Pierleoni family and the Frangipani family. In addition to the division of secular power, the cardinals themselves were split not only in their allegiances between the two families, but also along the fault line between older Gregorian cardinals and newer reformist cardinals who were not as concerned with the issues Gregory VII dealt with. The Frangipani family supported Lamberto, while the Pierleoni family supported Teobaldo. A majority of the cardinals elected Teobaldo pope, who took the name Celestine II, but just as he put on the red mantle, a group of Frangipani family members and supporters rushed into the church and wounded Celestine II, who resigned as a result of his wounds. Lamberto then was reelected pope by the cardinals and he took the name Honorius II. As a result of the *Concordat of Worms*, Honorius enjoyed a relative time of peace in which he could focus his attention on reforming the church. In 1128, he recognized the Knights Templar, a new religious order comprised of military monks—their rule was composed by St. Bernard of Clairvaux and they took vows of poverty, chastity, and obedience—whose purpose was to offer protection to Christian pilgrims travelling in the Holy Land. Honorius died on February 13, 1130.

Roman Intrigue, the Second Crusade, and the Rise of Frederick Barbarossa: Innocent II to Adrian IV (1130–1159)

Innocent II succeeded Honorius II on February 23, 1130. Like the election of his predecessor, the election of Innocent was filled with drama. The younger cardinals proclaimed Gregorio Papareschi pope, who took the name Innocent II, but the older Gregorian cardinals refused to recognize this election and elected Pietro Pierleoni, who took the name Anacletus II. Since the Pierleoni family occupied St. Peter's Basilica, Innocent had to be consecrated in another church, Santa Maria Nuovo in Campo Vincino. Politically, Anacletus had the upper hand at first because of the power of the Pierleoni family, but when Innocent fled to France, he was able to attract support from most of Europe thanks to the help of St. Bernard of Clairvaux, who threw his support behind Innocent. Soon, Innocent had all of France, England, and Germany supporting him. The schism that resulted from the double-election lasted for eight years until the death of Anacletus on January 1138. In 1139 at the Second Lateran Council, Innocent II annulled all of the acts of Anacletus. After various political conflicts with Louis VII and Roger II—Innocent had been forced to make a treaty with Roger in which the pope would recognize Roger as king of Sicily, and Roger would recognize Innocent as pope— Innocent died on September 24, 1143.

Celestine II succeeded Innocent II on October 3, 1143. Born Guido, Celestine reversed some of Innocent II's acts almost immediately. He was not pleased with the concessions Innocent had given to King Roger II of Sicily, and so did not ratify the treaty Roger made with Innocent II; however, he had to take a more moderate approach because of the pressure Roger was putting on the Papal States. Celestine died only after six months in office on March 8, 1144.

Lucius II succeeded Celestine II on March 12, 1144. The librarian of the Roman Church when he was elected pope, Lucius, born Gherardo Caccianemici dal Orso, had to navigate through a politically tumultuous sea. Lucius got into a conflict with Roger II of Sicily when he refused to give Robert some of the territory of the Papal States. After Roger III, Roger II's son, invaded Campania and attacked other portions of the Papal States, there was a treaty, but the ensuing peace only led to a resurgence of the Roman Senate. The brother of antipope Anacletus II headed the senate, which intended to strip the secular power from the papacy and the clergy. Lucius asked Roger II and Conrad III of Germany for aid, but did not receive any. Finally, Lucius decided that he had to protect the papacy and the clergy himself. He led a small army against the senate, but was injured by a large stone that had been thrown at him and died of his injuries on February 15, 1145.

Bl. Eugene III, who succeeded Lucius II on February 18, 1145, was the first Cistercian to become pope. In December 1145, after hearing about the fall of Edessa to the Muslims, Eugene announced the Second Crusade and instructed St. Bernard of Clairvaux, a fellow Cistercian, to preach the new crusade to the people. Eugene promoted monastic reform throughout Europe at various synods. When he returned to Rome, he was able to reach an agreement with the Romans with the assistance of Frederick I Barbarossa, the new German king. Eugene died of a fever on July 8, 1153, and his feast day is celebrated on July 8.

Anastasius IV succeeded Eugene III on July 12, 1153. An old man when elected pope, Anastasius enjoyed the good will and confidence of the Roman people, unlike his predecessors. Also unlike his predecessors, he was willing to bestow the pallium on the new archbishop of Magdeburg. He also restored the deposed archbishop of York, even though the Cistercians were opposed to him. Anastasius died on December 3, 1154.

Adrian IV, who succeeded Anastasius IV on December 4, 1154, was the first and only English pope. Born Nicholas Breakspear, Adrian immediately sought to take the power away from the senate by ousting Arnold of Brescia, the vehemently anti-papal leader of the senate. Before Palm Sunday of 1155, Adrian placed Rome under interdict—i.e. there would be no spiritual activities, which would cripple the local economy since Easter was on its way. The senate decided to exile Arnold and Adrian, and with the help of Frederick I Barbarossa, ensured that Arnold was executed. The Roman people offered the imperial crown to Frederick, and although he wanted to be emperor, he declined since "he considered that the empire came from God and his own strong right arm [and] . . . had no intention of accepting it from a bunch of middle-class radicals" (Duffy, 108). Frederick preferred to be crowned emperor by the pope himself, despite their differences. Eventually, Frederick was crowned by Adrian at St. Peter's on June 18, 1155. After countering a revolt of the Roman people who were upset with him for not accepting their offer to crown him emperor, Frederick went back to Germany. However, the relationship between Frederick and Adrian was still not mended. The two disputed several times over the next few years. The situation rapidly escalated. On one occasion, Adrian wrote a letter to Frederick in which he referred to the empire as a *beneficium* of the papacy, but the German word used to translate *beneficium* also meant feudal grants, which enraged the German court. The papal envoys, after escaping with their lives, informed Adrian. He then wrote another letter explaining that he did not mean any offense by using the word *beneficium*, but the damage had been done. Toward the end of Adrian's pontificate, he and the emperor were disputing northern territories in Italy. In fact, Adrian was threatening Frederick with excommunication, but before he could issue it, he died on September 1, 1159.

Conflict between Barbarossa and the Papacy and the Third Crusade: Alexander III to Celestine III (1159–1198)

Alexander III succeeded Adrian IV on September 20, 1159. Born Orlando, Alexander was a lawyer and a papal legate under Adrian IV. A small group of cardinals elected Cardinal Octavian pope, who took the name Victor IV, who thus became Frederick's antipope. In fact, Octavian's supporters took the red papal mantle from the newly elected pope's shoulders after breaking into a meeting, and Alexander had to flee to the Vatican fortress. King Louis VII of France and Henry II of England supported Alexander, while Frederick I Barbarossa of Germany sided with Victor. Because the emperor was against Alexander whose empire reached Italy, Alexander relocated to France from 1163 to 1165 and returned to Rome only after the Romans invited him back. After an alliance of northern Italian cities defeated Frederick, the emperor and pope entered into negotiations. They agreed that Alexander would lift Frederick's excommunication in return for Frederick's recognition that Alexander was the legitimate pope. In 1179 Alexander presided over the Third Lateran Council, which decreed that a two-thirds minimum vote was necessary for a papal candidate to become pope. Alexander died on August 30, 1181.

Lucius III succeeded Alexander III on September 1, 1181. The antipathy of the Romans forced him to have his coronation held at Velletri on September 6, 1181. A Cistercian monk and cardinal-bishop of Ostia when elected pope, Lucius was forced to live outside of Rome from March 1182 until the end of his pontificate in 1185. Lucius and Frederick unsuccessfully attempted to come to terms on three issues, namely a papal request for military aid against the Romans, Frederick's request that the pope crown his son and bless his marriage to Roger II's daughter, Constance, and a dispute with a countess over papal lands. Despite this failed attempt at an agreement, they were able to agree on a method for punishing heretics, who were to be excommunicated by the Church and transferred to the state so that they could be punished accordingly. This system was the forerunner to the inquisition. They also prepared for the Third Crusade to assist King Baldwin IV of Jerusalem, but Lucius died before they were completed on November 25, 1185.

Urban III succeeded Lucius III on November 25, 1185. Although he granted concessions to Frederick, such as swearing not to consecrate an anti-imperialist episcopal candidate for the archdiocese of Trier, and sending representatives to the wedding of Henry VI and Constance of Sicily, he nevertheless refused to crown Henry as co-emperor. When the pope broke his oath and consecrated the rival of the emperor's candidate for the episcopal see of Trier, Frederick was incensed. Frederick sent Henry to invade the Papal States and to surround the pope with troops, so that he could not be mobile, thus placing him virtually under house arrest. Eventually Urban gave in, but shortly after he planned on excommunicating Frederick. Before he could do so however, he died on October 20, 1187.

Gregory VIII succeeded Urban III on October 25, 1187. Already quite old when he was elected pope, perhaps eighty-seven years old, Gregory was pope for less than two months. His pontificate was marked by a much more conciliatory approach toward the emperor than those of his predecessors. After Gregory wrote letters to the emperor which were intended to ameliorate the relationship between Frederick and the papacy, Frederick lifted the virtual house arrest. Gregory then called for the Third Crusade after he heard the news that the Kingdom of Jerusalem had been defeated and captured by Muslim forces at the Battle of Hattin. Seeing the Muslim conquest of Jerusalem as a sign that God was not happy with the Christians on account of their sins, Gregory ordered that all the Crusaders should wear penitential garb. He also attempted to reform the clergy by forbidding them to wear opulent attire and to take up arms. Before he could see the beginning of the Third Crusade, Gregory died on December 17, 1187.

Clement III succeeded Gregory VIII on December 19, 1187. Clement brought about a state of peace between the papacy and the Roman commune that enabled him to return the papacy to Rome. Clement established his residency in the Lateran after the Romans allowed him to return in February 1188. According to Richard McBrien, "The senators acknowledged his sovereignty and restored papal revenues and the right to mint coins. In return, Clement II had to make substantial annual and special-occasion payments to the commune and leave the administration of the city largely to them" (208). With peace restored, the Papal States were handed back to Clement III and Clement agreed to crown Henry VI as co-emperor. However, Clement died before Henry arrived in Rome. Essentially agreeing with Gregory VIII's perspective that the Crusader loss of Jerusalem was a sign of God's judgment, Clement reinforced Gregory's injunction that Crusaders wear penitential garb. He also had preachers travel throughout Europe to encourage peace among Christian kingdoms. Frederick I Barbarossa, who organized the Third Crusade, died on the way to the Third Crusade in Asia Minor, by drowning in a river in 1190. Clement III died shortly after on March 20, 1191.

Celestine III, who was eighty-five when he was elected pope, succeeded Clement III on April 14, 1191. The aged pontiff crowned Henry VI emperor on April 15. Henry, apparently not as noble as his father, arbitrarily appointed bishops—thus reopening the issue of investiture, had a bishop murdered, and put Richard the Lionheart in prison. Celestine, already old, took no actions against Henry, who died on September 28, 1197. In December 1197, Celestine, who was now in his nineties, offered to resign if the cardinals were willing to elect his friend to the papacy, but the cardinals declined his offer. Celestine died on January 8, 1198.

Frederick II and the Fourth and Fifth Crusades: Innocent III to Gregory IX (1198–1241)

Innocent III, "one of the most important and powerful popes in the entire history of the Church" (McBrien, 209), succeeded Celestine III on February 22, 1198. He claimed authority over both spiritual and temporal realms, and emphatically resorted to the use of the title "Vicar of Christ." Elected pope at the age of thirty-seven, Innocent was a vigorous pontiff. He replaced public officials in Rome with pro-papal officials and expanded the territory of the Papal States. With the death of Henry VI, Innocent had to deal with the question of imperial succession. Otto of Brunswick and Frederick of Sicily, both contended for the imperial crown and appealed to the pope to arbitrate between their claims. Innocent ruled in favor of Otto, but when Otto invaded the Papal States, Innocent excommunicated and deposed him, and transferred the imperial crown to Frederick. He also intervened in a number of other issues. Innocent's ecclesiastical agenda included the Fourth Crusade, the reform of the Church, and the combatting of heresy, in particular Albigensianism.

The Fourth Crusade, which occurred between 1202 and 1204, was ultimately a disaster. The Crusaders sacked Constantinople in 1204, an act which severely increased Constantinople's antipathy towards Rome.

In 1209, St. Francis of Assisi arrived in Rome with his original followers to request permission from Innocent III to start a new order. Although Innocent was not convinced at first of the merit of a possible new Franciscan order, he changed his mind after he had a dream of St. Francis holding up the toppling Lateran basilica in 1210. He sent the Franciscans to preach throughout Europe and gave permission to St. Dominic, the founder of the Dominicans, to debate with the Albigensians publicly. However, when the papal legate, Pierre de Castelnau, was murdered in 1208, Innocent called for a crusade against the heretics. Simon de Montfort launched the Albigensian Crusade, which resulted in much bloodshed.

The Fourth Lateran Council was held in 1215. Among the council's decrees, the Eucharist was defined theologically by the transubstantiation doctrine, the founding of new religious orders was condemned, and all Christians were to observe a truce in preparation for the next crusade, the Fifth Crusade, which was scheduled to begin in 1217.

Innocent's reign would presumably have lasted much, much longer had he been in good health, and not died unexpectedly of a fever on July 16, 1216, at the age of fifty-five or fifty-six.

His papacy set the tone for the papacy for the rest of the thirteenth century.

Honorius III succeeded Innocent III on July 24, 1216. With the commencement of the Fifth Crusade fast approaching, Honorius worked hard to get the crusade in order for its scheduled date. The Fifth Crusade, like the Fourth Crusade, was a failure. The pope crowned Frederick II as emperor in 1220 with the hope that he would participate in the next crusade, but instead had to resort to the threat of excommunication to get Frederick to participate. Honorius approved the Dominican rule in 1216, the Franciscan rule in 1223, and the Carmelite rule in 1226; the Dominicans, Franciscans, and Carmelites were the last orders formed before the Fourth Lateran Council, which prohibited the formation of new religious orders. A knowledgeable theologian, Honorius wrote a collection of decretals, which are considered to be the first official book of canon law, and wrote biographies of Celestine III and Gregory VII. Honorius died on March 18, 1227.

Gregory IX, the nephew of Innocent III, succeeded Honorius III on March 19, 1227. Most famous—or infamous for establishing the Papal Inquisition, Gregory strongly supported the Dominicans and Franciscans. He put together a collection of papal decretals that became the primary source of canon law, and reopened the University of Paris in 1231 after there had been a strike there in 1229.

Frederick, who had been threatened with excommunication by Honorius III if he did not embark on the crusade by 1227, set off in August of 1227, but informed Honorius that he had to return to port because he was ill. Judging this a pretext, Honorius excommunicated Frederick, who set sail in 1228 regardless of his excommunication. Instead of fighting, Frederick managed to come to an agreement with al-Kamil and secured Jerusalem for the Christians. Upset that the crusade should be led by someone who had been excommunicated, Honorius refused to lift it, even when he heard that Frederick had successfully recaptured Jerusalem through diplomacy. Honorius then attempted to set up a rival king in Germany and sought to set up an army that would withstand the imperial forces, but Frederick crushed it as soon as he returned in 1230. A month later, a truce was forged between the pope and the emperor according to which Frederick promised not to encroach on the Papal States, and the pope lifted Frederick's excommunication.

Relations with Frederick broke down in 1238 when Frederick conquered the Lombard League and it became obvious that he was determined to conquer all of Italy. Gregory excommunicated Frederick in 1239 for invading Sardinia, and Frederick then called a council at which he denounced the pope. Both the pope and the emperor resorted to name-calling and propaganda, with Gregory calling Frederick "the forerunner of the Antichrist" and a "monster of calumny," and Frederick calling Gregory a "Pharisee seated on the chair of pestilence, anointed with the oil of wickedness" (McBrien, 213-214). Frederick mobilized his forces, invaded the Papal States, and surrounded the Eternal City. Gregory died on August 22, 1241, with Rome practically in the hands of Frederick II, but the emperor's forces withdrew after Gregory died and Frederick decided to wait and see what would happen.

The End of the Hohenstaufen Dynasty: Celestine IV to Clement IV (1241–1268)

Celestine IV succeeded Gregory IX on October 25, 1241, but was on the Chair of Peter for a very short time. His pontificate was possibly the second shortest in history, behind Urban VII, who was pope for twelve days in 1590. With only ten remaining cardinals after the death of Gregory IX—there were two others in prison—a unanimous decision was impossible since some cardinals supported the anti-imperialist policies of Gregory IX and others were utterly opposed to them. Finally, Goffredo Castiglioni was elected pope and took the name Celestine IV, but died two weeks later on November 10, 1241.

Innocent IV, a brilliant canon lawyer, succeeded Celestine IV on June 28, 1243. A man with a utilitarian outlook, Innocent was nepotistic and helped himself to the church's funds. He also has the unenviable distinction of being the first pope who approved the use of torture to extract confessions from people accused of heresy. Knowing that the situation with Frederick II was precarious, Innocent fled Rome and sought refuge under the aegis of King Louis IX of France. In 1245, Innocent held the First Council of Lyon. For Innocent, the Council needed to address the following five issues, which he called the five "wounds" of the Church: "the sins of the clergy, the loss of Jerusalem to Islam (since 1244), the troubles of the Latin kingdom of Constantinople, the Mongol invasion of

Europe, and the persecution of the Church by Frederick"
(Duffy, 116). The council promptly excommunicated and
deposed Frederick for perjury, heresy, and a number of other
crimes. Frederick's excommunication was renewed by
Innocent in 1248. After the death of Frederick II in 1250,
Innocent felt more at ease and went back to Rome in 1251.
There was one more conflict that Innocent faced before he
died, and that was his conflict with Conrad IV, Frederick II's
son, over Sicily. The pope wanted Sicily as papal land, but
Conrad would not let him acquire it. After Conrad died in
1254, Innocent annexed Sicily. He died in Naples on December
7, 1254.

Alexander IV, the nephew of Gregory IX, succeeded Innocent
IV on December 12, 1254. Residing primarily in Viterbo,
Alexander struggled against Manfred, the illegitimate son of
Frederick II, who led a revolt in Sicily. After excommunicating
Manfred, Alexander attempted to recapture Sicily by force of
arms, but failed. In 1258, Alexander instituted a canon stating
that the Inquisition was not to investigate accusations of
sorcery—unless heresy was also involved—since sorcery was
to be considered a secular offense; as a result, trials of
witchcraft later were primarily a Protestant phenomenon

(Selwood). The pope also canonized St. Clare of Assisi, who died in 1253. Alexander IV died on May 25, 1261.

Urban IV succeeded Alexander IV on August 29, 1261. A man of humble origins, the son of a shoemaker, Jacques Pantaléon was the patriarch of Jerusalem before he had been elected pope. Since there were only eight cardinals at the time of his election, he immediately created fourteen new cardinals, six of whom were French, like himself. Urban sought to purge Italy of the power of the Hohenstaufen dynastythe family of Frederick II, and was able to regain the portions of the Papal States Alexander had lost, but was forced to enter into negotiations with Manfred when he attacked the Papal States. Urban died on October 2, 1264. Pope Urban IV is known for making the feast of Corpus Christi a feast of the universal Church and for commissioning St. Thomas Aquinas (1225–1274) to write liturgical texts for it; this was in response to the renaissance of the doctrine of transubstantiation, which had been defined at the Fourth Lateran Council in 1215 under Innocent III.

Clement IV succeeded Urban IV on February 5, 1265. Born Guy Foulques, he was a soldier, a lawyer, and secretary to King St. Louis IX, as well as a married man with two daughters. After his wife died, he was ordained and quickly became bishop, archbishop, and cardinal. Elected pope *in absentia*, he chose the name Clement IV and disguised himself as a monk so he could return to Italy safely. When he arrived in Italy, he installed Charles of Anjou as king of Sicily and Naples instead of Manfred. In 1266, after raising a large amount of money, Clement hired a French army to defeat Manfred, whom they killed. Charles of Anjou was not popular with the people however, and Conradin, the king of Jerusalem and last of the Hohenstaufens, marched on Italy. Although Conradin was welcomed by the Romans, Clement deposed and excommunicated him before Charles of Anjou captured and beheaded him after a trial. In regard to Rome's relationship with Constantinople, Clement attempted to reconcile with the East, but his prerequisites for reunification were deemed unacceptable. Clement IV died on November 29, 1268.

With the end of the Hohenstaufen dynasty, the house of Angevin became the dominant family. A powerful Charles of Anjou, the representative of that house, was in the backyard of the Papal States. The alliance between Clement IV and Charles of Anjou was understandable since Charles was Louis IX's brother; Clement felt obligated to Louis since it was due to

Louis that he had become a cardinal. But with a new power, came new threats.

The Angevin Rule of Sicily and Its Decline:
Bl. Gregory X to Nicholas IV (1272–1292)

Bl. Gregory X succeeded Clement IV on March 27, 1272. The papal election for a successor to Clement IV had been moving at a snail's pace from 1268. In 1271 St. Bonaventure, the minister general of the Franciscans, advised that the cardinals should be locked in the papal palace at Viterbo and threatened with starvation if they did not choose a successor quickly. The cardinals still took a while, sustaining themselves with bread and water that was given to them through the roof of the palace. Born Teobaldo Visconti, Gregory was elected *in absentia* since he was on a crusade at Acre in the Holy Land with King Edward I of England, Edward Longshanks, serving as an archdeacon. After he was elected pope, Gregory made his way back to Rome after five months and was ordained as a priest and a bishop.

Once he was consecrated bishop, Gregory made it a priority to free the churches and holy sites in the Holy Land, and sought to reunify the Greek and Roman churches. In order to accomplish these goals, he called the Second Council of Lyon, which met in 1274. While the council came up with a system to finance the crusade, it never occurred. The plan to reunify the East and West was seemingly a success. The Greek delegates of Michael VIII Palaeologus—who had taken Constantinople and ended the Latin Empire that began as a result of the sack of Constantinople during the Fourth Crusade during Innocent III's pontificate—accepted the *Filioque*, assented to the primacy of the Holy See, and celebrated Mass with Gregory. Although the unification was ratified, most of the Byzantine Christians refused to accept it. Another council act was to make changes to the election process in papal conclaves. This included requiring cardinals to assemble in the town where the pope died within ten days of death, prohibiting cardinals from having contact with the outside world during this time, and making living conditions more austere as the papal election continued. Gregory X died on January 10, 1276, of a fever as he was travelling through northern Italy, and his feast day is celebrated on January 9.

Bl. Innocent V, the first Dominican pope, succeeded Bl. Gregory X on January 21, 1276. The papal custom of wearing a white cassock could have started with Innocent since he wore his Dominican habit while he was pope. A renowned theologian, Innocent had worked with St. Albert the Great and St. Thomas Aquinas to put together a curriculum for the Dominicans (Kelly, 199) and was a friend of St. Bonaventure, whose funeral sermon he preached. Innocent had a different perspective on Charles of Anjou than his predecessors did. After confirming Charles's senatorial role in Rome, Innocent turned his attention to launching a new crusade. One of his political mistakes was to reveal to Michael VIII Palaeologus that Charles was planning to recapture Constantinople since it had been violently wrested from the Latins. In addition to this, he sent messengers to demand that the Greeks accept the *filioque* and papal primacy, but before they arrived, Innocent V died on June 22, 1276. His feast day is June 22.

Adrian V succeeded Bl. Innocent V on July 11, 1276. Although he was elected pope, he died before he was ordained a priest. At the time, election was canonically sufficient for a person to be pope, so his election was canonically valid, but according to the 1983 Code of Canon Law, episcopal consecration is essential for one to be recognized as pope. Adrian V died at Viterbo on August 18, 1276, just five weeks after he was elected pope.

John XXI, the only Portuguese pope, succeeded Adrian V on September 8, 1276. He was also the only medical doctor to have been a pope. Since there was confusion about the numbering, John counted himself as XXI instead of XX even though there was no John XX. John had been Bl. Gregory X's physician and had taught medicine at the University of Siena. An academic-minded person, like Innocent V, John wrote books on logic, the soul, and ophthalmology. John left most of the decision-making to Cardinal Giovanni Gaetano, who later became Pope Nicholas III, and retired to a study that he ordered constructed in the papal palace at Viterbo. The construction was faulty and when the roof fell on John, he died of his injuries a few days later on May 20, 1277.

Nicholas III succeeded John XXI on December 26, 1277. After he was elected, Nicholas took up residence at the Vatican Palace, the first pope to do so. Politically astute, Nicholas set out to increase the Holy See's political clout and independence in Italy. To this effect, Nicholas persuaded Charles of Anjou to step down as senator of Rome when his term expired, and he set himself up as a senator of Rome for life. He also decreed that no one could become a senator of Rome without first receiving papal approval. After negotiations with King Rudolf I, Nicholas acquired disputed lands in Romagna, thus increasing the size of the Papal States. On the ecclesiastical front, Nicholas promoted Franciscans and Dominicans to powerful positions. He also unsuccessfully attempted to mend the division between the East and the West. Nicholas's contemporaries accused him of nepotism, for which he was placed in Hell in Dante's *Inferno*. He died on August 22, 1280.

Martin IV succeeded Nicholas III on March 23, 1281, although he was actually the second Pope Martin—Marinus I and II were listed as Martin II and III. Martin reversed his predecessor's policies by giving his senatorial position to Charles of Anjou. He also supported Charles's plans to recapture Constantinople through force, and excommunicated Michael VIII Palaeologus—even though he had been extremely accommodating to the demands of the Holy See. The formula of union between the East and the West established at the Second Council of Lyon was de facto abrogated, and the plans to recapture Constantinople were stymied when a group of rebels sought to overthrow the French control of Sicily in 1282. The rebels offered the island to the pope, but Martin refused and encouraged them to recognize Charles as their leader. Ecclesiastically, his bias toward the French—despite his own French roots, alienated many Catholics, especially the Germans. Martin died on March 28, 1285.

Honorius IV succeeded Martin IV on May 20, 1285. Elderly when elected, Honorius a grandnephew of Honorius III, sought to reclaim Sicily for the Angevins, but was not able to do so. When the reigning king of Sicily, Peter III, died, his son James claimed the throne of Sicily. Honorius excommunicated him when he heard the news. But when Charles of Anjou's heir, Charles II of Salerno, forfeited his claim to Sicily in order to obtain James's release from prison, Honorius could do nothing about it although it made him "furious" (Kelly, 204). He courted Rudolf in order to set up a political alliance, hoping to crown him in Rome, but Rudolf had to postpone the trip. Ultimately, the coronation never took place. In ecclesiastical matters, Honorius strongly supported the Dominicans and Franciscans and encouraged the study of oriental languages at the University of Paris, hoping that it would facilitate the reconciliation between the East and the West. Honorius IV died in April 1287.

Nicholas IV, the first Franciscan pope, succeeded Honorius IV on February 22, 1288. He was St. Bonaventure's successor as the general of the Franciscan order. The first time he was elected on February 15, he declined, but when he was elected again on February 22, he accepted. Nicholas showed extreme favoritism toward the Colonna family and as a result, was not permitted to reside in Rome in peace. Although his political ventures had little effect, on the ecclesiastical front, he sent a Franciscan missionary to the court of Kubla Khan in China and sent other missionaries to the Balkans, Persia, the Near East, and Ethiopia. He is also known for bringing talented artists to Rome to beautify its churches. Nicholas died on April 4, 1292.

King Philip IV of France and the Colonna Family: St. Celestine V to Bl. Benedict XI (1294–1304)

St. Celestine V, famous for resigning from the papacy, succeeded Nicholas IV on August 29, 1294. Before he was elected to the papacy he had been a hermit. With the cardinals unable to reach a two-thirds majority vote after twenty-seven months of vacancy, the dean of the College of Cardinals cited a prophecy by hermit Pietro del Murrone that the cardinals would be under God's wrath if they did not hasten to elect a pope. The dean made it known that he would cast his vote for Pietro and eventually all of the cardinals voted for him. He was consecrated as bishop of Rome in Naples where he was essentially the puppet of Charles II. An uneducated man, Celestine was politically and ecclesiastically inept despite his great piety. When his proposal to fast and pray while three cardinals took charge of ecclesiastical affairs was rejected, he decided to resign with the help of Cardinal Benedetto Caetani, a canon lawyer, who ended up succeeding Celestine V. The resignation took effect on December 13, 1294, less than four months after Celestine became pope.

Boniface VIII succeeded Celestine V on January 23, 1295. In McBrien's estimation, Boniface VIII was "one of the three most powerful medieval popes, along with Gregory VII (1073–85) and Innocent III (1198-1216)" (229). Fearing that a schism might occur since Celestine was still alive, instead of allowing him to return to his hermitage, he put Celestine in a castle tower where he died in 1296. He also annulled most of Celestine's acts. His contributions to canon law were immense, but Boniface was more concerned with political matters than matters pertaining to the soul. He unsuccessfully attempted to get Charles II back on the throne of Sicily, and tried to hammer out a peace agreement between England and France, but this merely led to a conflict between Boniface and Philip IV of France. After writing a bull against Philip to stop his practice of taxing the clergy to finance his wars, Philip ceased France's exports of gold and other valuables to the Holy See. Boniface backed off and sealed a brief peace between himself and Philip by canonizing Philip's grandfather, St. Louis IX.

On the domestic front Boniface came into conflict with the Colonna family, which had initially supported his bid to the papacy. Disillusioned by his high-handed rule and his Sicilian policy, they started to question the legitimacy of Celestine V's resignation.

Boniface declared the year 1300 as a year of Jubilee, the first Holy Year in the Catholic Church, and granted plenary indulgences to the Roman pilgrims. In response to another conflict with Philip, Boniface wrote *Unam sanctam*, another papal bull, in which he claimed that the Church wields both the temporal and spiritual powers and that secular powers are judged by the spiritual. Philip, backed by the Colonna family, attacked Boniface with numerous accusations including simony, heresy, usurping the papacy, and sexual misconduct. While he was preparing to promulgate a bull of excommunication against Philip, Boniface was arrested at Anagni where he had been born, by the king's men, but was rescued by the citizens of Anagni. With the Orsini family escorting him, Boniface made his way back to Rome, but died of a fever on September 25, 1303. Dante Alighieri, one of Boniface's staunchest opponents, placed Boniface in the eighth circle of Hell for simony in his *Inferno*, the first part of his *Divine Comedy*.

Bl. Benedict XI succeeded Boniface VIII on October 22, 1303. A Dominican, he took the name of Benedict XI, since Benedict X had not yet been considered an antipope. One of the few cardinals who stood by Boniface VIII, Benedict is often described as a weak pontiff despite his erudition. He sought to appease the various disgruntled parties in the aftermath of Boniface's autocratic rule. In France, Philip IV was still proceeding with a council in which he planned to condemn

Boniface. Benedict absolved Philip of every accusation Boniface threw at him, pardoned everyone except the leader of those who had participated in Boniface's arrest at Anagni, and granted Philip tithes from the clergy for two years. All of these acts eventually appeased the wrath of Philip. Benedict died on July 7, 1304, and his feast day is July 7.

The brief and inept papacy of Celestine V paved the way for one of the most powerful popes in the Middle Ages, Boniface VIII, who attracted the fury of King Philip IV of France. Boniface's successor, Benedict XI, strove to undo the offence that his predecessor had caused the king, but Philip continued to exercise his sway over the papacy. The next pope, Clement V, eventually resided in Avignon, France, where the next six popes—all French, like Clement—resided until 1378. This period of history is known as the Avignon Papacy, or the Babylonian Captivity of the Papacy.

The Avignon Papacy:
Clement V to Gregory XI (1305–1378)

Clement V succeeded Benedict XI on June 5, 1305. Born Raymond Bertrand de Got, Clement V, who was archbishop of Bordeaux at the time of his election, was elected pope after a long conclave of eleven months in which the pro-French, anti-Boniface cardinals were deadlocked with the pro-Boniface cardinals, who were against King Philip IV. The position of the pro-Boniface cardinals weakened when they split up, and Raymond, a Frenchman, was subsequently elected pope. Although he wanted to be crowned at Vienne, Philip had Clement come to Lyon for his coronation. Overtly nepotistic, Clement made four of his nephews a cardinal a month after his consecration, and created a total of ten cardinals—nine of whom were French. Clement stopped at various French cities for a few years until 1309 when he settled in Avignon since it did not belong directly to Philip, but to the Angevin kings of Naples. This marked the beginning of the Avignon Papacy, a period of time that lasted until 1378, when all the popes were French and resided in France instead of Rome. Philip had Clement annul all the anti-French acts of Boniface VIII, ensured that the gang leader who forcefully attacked Boniface was exonerated, and engineered the canonization of Celestine V, who was canonized in 1313.

Greedy for more power, Philip next went after the Knights Templar. He arrested them and extracted forced confessions. After this, Philip demanded that Clement dissolve the order, which he reluctantly did at the Council of Vienne. Although the Templars' wealth was handed over to the Hospitallers, it effectively went into the possession of Philip. Clement V died of stomach cancer on April 20, 1314.

John XXII succeeded Clement V on August 7, 1316. Born Jacques Duèse, he was elected when he was seventy-two years old and was most likely intended to be a transitional pope. His papacy, however, lasted for eighteen years until John was almost ninety years old! John was a capable administrator and able to regain financial stability in the Church, which Clement V had jeopardized in his papacy. Like Clement, John was nepotistic and manifested a strong French bias; every one of his appointments for cardinals were French except five.

John entered into a conflict with Louis IV who became the Holy Roman Emperor in 1323. Louis sided with the Spiritual Franciscans in their debate about poverty with the Conventional Franciscans, whom John sided with. William of Occam, the Franciscan philosopher, advocated the Spiritual Franciscans' view and was an ally of Louis. John excommunicated Louis and Louis condemned the pope, burned an effigy of him, and installed an antipope, Nicholas V, who eventually repented, went to Avignon, and received a pardon from John.

In a series of four sermons John XXII delivered at the end of 1331 and the beginning of 1332, John claimed that the blessed would not see God until after the final judgment, which was opposed to the view traditionally held that the saints would see God immediately after death. John's opponents jumped on this misstep and quickly condemned him of heresy. On his death bed, John changed his view and said that it was merely his personal opinion instead of official teaching. He died on December 4, 1334.

Benedict XII succeeded John XXII on January 8, 1335. Known for being a learned theologian and skilled inquisitor, the cardinals perhaps chose Benedict since they wanted a professional theologian instead of an amateur like John XXII (Kelly, 217). Benedict initially considered moving the papacy back to Rome when a contingency from Italy encouraged him to make the move. He even spent money on maintaining St. Peter's and the Lateran, but since the French king and most of the cardinals were against the move, and the political environment in Italy did not seem to be favorable to the papacy, he changed his mind. Benedict brought about some strict reforms primarily concerning ecclesiastical posts. He thought that clerics should remain at the posts to which they were assigned—it is ironic that he was at Avignon instead of Rome, and that monks should stay in their monasteries instead of wandering listlessly. A Cistercian himself before he was elected pope, he counteracted simony and sought to regulate the power and authority of various religious orders including the Benedictines, Cistercians, and Franciscans, and emphasized regular visitations. Politically, Benedict was unable to prevent the Hundred Years' War and acquired hostility from the English for his blatant support of the French. He died on April 25, 1342.

Clement VI succeeded Benedict XII on May 7, 1342. Born Pierre Roger, Clement, a Benedictine before he was elected pope, was known for being more relaxed than his austere predecessor. He was also encouraged to move the papacy back to Rome but refused. However, he did call for a Jubilee year in 1350, which helped improve the Roman economy. Drawn to lavishness, Clement depleted the papal treasury that had been built up by John XXII and Benedict XII. In order to restock the treasury, he imposed new taxes and sought new ways to acquire revenue. He was also known for shameless nepotism. One good point of his papacy, is that he defended the Jews when they were accused of being responsible for the Black Death. Clement VI died on December 6, 1352.

Innocent VI succeeded Clement VI on December 18, 1352. Born Etienne Aubert, Innocent VI followed Benedict XII's pattern of zealous reform. He opted for a simpler lifestyle for the papal court, and like John XXII, was especially severe in his dealings with the Spiritual Franciscans. Although he hoped to move back to Rome, he was not able to because of the political and financial circumstances he found himself in. The Hundred Years' War resumed and when there was a truce, Innocent had to bribe restless marauders to keep them from plundering Avignon. In addition, he was unable to reunite the Latin and Greek churches since the Greeks' offer to submit themselves to the Holy See hinged upon military assistance against the Turks, and there were not enough funds in the papal treasury to help them. Innocent VI died on September 12, 1362.

Bl. Urban V succeeded Innocent VI on November 6, 1362. Described as the best Avignon pope (McBrien, 243), Abbot Guillaume de Grimoard was a Benedictine monk who was a canon lawyer, but not a cardinal, when he was elected pope on

September 28, 1362. Opting to forego the traditional pomp of the papal enthronement and coronation, he continued in the vein of Innocent VI by reducing the luxury of the papal court even further. He also chose to keep his black Benedictine habit and strict rule of life. He used up the papal treasury by supporting students, colleges, architects, and artists. Urban had great ambitions of launching another crusade to liberate the holy sites and of restoring communion with the Greeks, but was unable to accomplish either goal. He was able to go back to Rome briefly despite the pressure of the French cardinals to stay in Avignon. In 1367 Urban arrived in Rome and ordered that repairs be done to some of the dilapidated churches. Urban crowned Charles IV's wife empress and met with John V Palaeologus, the Byzantine emperor. Although John became Catholic, no reunification occurred. The Greek bishops urged Urban to call an ecumenical council, but instead of calling one, he attempted to deal with the matter by establishing a Latin Church in the East.

The French cardinals were still pressuring Urban to move back to Avignon. With the political situation heating up with the Hundred Years' War and skirmishes flaring up in the Italian countryside, Urban eventually heeded the wish of the cardinals, despite a prophecy by St. Bridget of Sweden that he would die early if he decided to return to Avignon. Less than two years after his return to Avignon on September 27, 1370, Bl. Urban V died on June 5, 1372.

Gregory XI succeeded Urban V on January 4, 1371, at the age of forty-two. Born Pierre Roger de Beaufort, Pierre became a cardinal at the age of eighteen or nineteen through the appointment of his uncle, Clement VI. Only a deacon at the time of his election, Gregory was ordained a priest and then a bishop five days after he was elected pope. St. Catherine of Sienna ultimately persuaded Gregory to return the papacy to Rome in spite of protests from his cardinals and relatives. He eventually made the journey back to Rome on January 17, 1377, but had to retreat to Anagni in the wake of political turmoil in Rome where he died on March 2, 1378. The long sixty-nine-year exile of the papacy from Rome in Avignon, dubbed the Babylonian Captivity of the Papacy, had finally come to an end.

The Great Western Schism:
Urban VI to Gregory XII (1378–1415)

Urban VI, the last non-cardinal to be elected pope, succeeded Gregory XI on April 8, 1378. Born Bartolomeo Prignano, he was the first pope to be elected in a Roman conclave since 1303. There hadn't been a non-French pope since before the Avignon Papacy, but the Romans demanded an Italian pope during the conclave and rioting ensued. Cardinal Prignano was considered a capable administrator since he had served the Curia for twenty years.

However, the cardinals were shocked at the new pope's attitude upon assuming the papacy. Apparently, the power of the papacy got to Urban's head, and he went off on tyrannical tirades and verbally abused the cardinals who were responsible for electing him. The French cardinals attempted to come to some agreement with the pope, but after it became apparent that he was utterly intransigent and drunk with power, they published a decree declaring Urban's election to be invalid and electing an antipope, Clement VII, who was the cousin of the French king, thus inaugurating the Great Western Schism.

The two claimants to the papal throne divided Europe along sharp lines. Urban and Clement excommunicated each other and then sent troops to attack each other. Urban's army overcame Clement's and captured the castle where he was residing, after which Clement fled to Avignon where he set up an opulent papal court. While the feuding between Urban and Clement died down, Urban, convinced of the legitimacy of his pontificate, declined to resolve the situation with Clement. Instead, Urban turned his sights to benefiting his relatives; in particular, he was busy acquiring the kingdom of Naples for his nephew. He also excommunicated and deposed Queen Joanna in 1380 for supporting his nemesis, Clement VII, and crowned his cousin, Charles of Durazzo, king. Realizing that his cousin was on the verge of insanity, Charles plotted with some of the cardinals to depose Urban, but when the pope found out about this, he preached a crusade against Charles and tortured and executed the cardinals who had plotted against him. Urban left the Papal States in great turmoil when he died, probably of poisoning, on October 15, 1389.

Boniface IX succeeded Urban VI on November 9, 1389. A man with a congenial personality, Pietro Tomacelli was benevolent despite his nepotistic and simoniacal activities. Upon Boniface's election, Clement VII excommunicated him and Boniface in turn excommunicated the antipope. When Boniface discovered a plot against him in Rome, he abolished the Rome's republican government and claimed absolute authority of the city. When Clement VII died, King Charles VI of France urged the cardinals in Avignon not to elect a successor, but before the cardinals received the letter, they elected Cardinal Pedro de Luna who called himself Benedict XIII. Boniface, a skilled administrator, infamously sold church offices to the highest bidder and sold indulgences so as to increase the papacy's revenue. Pope Boniface IX died on October 1, 1404.

Innocent VII succeeded Boniface IX on October 17, 1404. Although he had promised to do everything in his power to end the schism if elected, he refused to meet with Benedict XIII. There was civil unrest in Rome, which Innocent quelled by seeking aid from Ladislas, the king of Naples. When a second civil unrest erupted in Rome, Innocent's nephew murdered eleven citizens, which caused the infuriated mob to storm the Vatican. Innocent had to flee to Viterbo, but was welcomed back in Rome in March of 1406. Innocent died on November 6, 1406.

Gregory XII succeeded Innocent VII on December 19, 1406. During the conclave, Angelo Correr, along with the other cardinals, swore that if one from among their group was elected pope, he would abdicate if the Avignon antipope,

Benedict XIII, was willing to abdicate, and that the new pope would not create any new cardinals. When Correr was elected pope however, he created four cardinals after it became apparent that Benedict XIII was unwilling to abdicate. In response to the pope breaking his pre-election oath, the vast majority of cardinals met on March 25, 1409, at the Council of Pisa. On June 5, they deposed Gregory XII and Benedict XIII as schismatics, perjurers, and heretics. They declared the Chair of Peter vacant, after which they elected a new pope, an antipope, Alexander V. When Alexander died, the Council of Pisa elected Cardinal Baldassare Cossa pope, who took the name John XXIII. After John XXIII was deposed at the Council of Constance on May 29, 1415, the council sought Gregory's abdication, which Gregory was willing to consider, as long as the council would allow him to preside. The council agreed and Gregory abdicated on July 4, 1415, and died at the age of ninety on October 18, 1417. Benedict XIII was deposed by the unified Rome and Avignon cardinals. The Great Western Schism had finally come to an end and the next pontificate would signify a return to normalcy.

The Transition into the Renaissance: Martin V to Callixtus III (1417–1458)

Martin V succeeded Gregory XII on November 21, 1417. The conclave that had elected Oddo Colonna on the feast of St. Martin was unusual, since it was the first and last conclave since 1058 to include lay electors with thirty representatives from five nations along with twenty-two cardinals. A deacon before he became pope, the newly elected pope was ordained a priest and consecrated a bishop shortly after his election. Not allowing himself to be persuaded to move the papacy to Germany or Avignon, Martin made his way to Rome slowly but surely, stopping in Mantua and Florence along the way for long periods of time before arriving in Rome on September 28, 1420. After Martin's papal troops defeated Braccione di Montone in 1424 and put down a revolt at Bologna in 1429, the pope was able to restructure the Papal States and make use of the papal treasury, which had been lost. Martin's ecclesiastical affairs proved to be less successful than his political endeavors. He was unable to progress toward the reunification of the Greek and Latin churches and was unsuccessful at mounting a crusade against John Hus's followers in Bohemia. To Martin's credit however, he showed great understanding toward the Jews by condemning anti-Jewish preaching and forbidding the forced baptism of Jewish children. Martin died on February 20, 1431.

Eugene IV, the nephew of Gregory XII, succeeded Martin V on March 11, 1431. He had been a monk before he became pope. One of Eugene's first moves was a political move against the Colonna family, the family of Martin V, since Martin had given so much land and gifts to his nephews and relatives. Eugene essentially sought to wrest the territories of the Papal States from the hands of the Colonnas. Since the Council of Constance had previously claimed that an ecumenical council had more authority than the pope, Eugene was suspicious of the Council of Basel's activities, and he attempted to dissolve it under the pretext of poor attendance. The council, however, would not disperse, appealing to the ruling of the Council of Constance on the superiority of an ecumenical council. A schism was narrowly avoided through the diplomacy of King Sigismund, and Eugene had to retract the bull in which he declared the council dissolved. During this time, the Colonna family had been stoking revolt in the countryside, which broke out in May 1434. Eugene escaped by disguising himself and fleeing to Florence.

Eugene wanted to reunify the Latin and Greek Churches. Although the Greeks initially wanted the council at Constantinople, they agreed to have it in Ferrara. Eugene had a fleet transport the emperor and patriarch, along with a

Byzantine delegation, to Ferrara where the council opened on April 9, 1438. It met again in January in Florence on account of the plague. A reunification was reached and accepted by John VIII Palaeologus, Patriarch Joseph II, and nearly all of the Eastern bishops. The terms of the reunion included the acceptance of the doctrine of Purgatory and papal primacy, and a recognition of the legitimacy of both the use of unleavened bread at Mass and the *Filioque* in the creed. Eugene was able to sign agreements with the Armenians, Copts, Chaldeans, and Maronites. Although the Eastern bishops accepted the terms, the monks and the populace in the East did not, and the Latin and Greek Churches ultimately remained divided.

The Council of Basel deposed Eugene and elected an antipope, Felix V, who was a layman. Felix V was the last antipope in history with a strong backing. Eugene died on February 23, 1447, regretting the day he left the monastery.

Nicholas V succeeded Eugene IV on March 6, 1447. Born Tommaso Parentucelli, he is often described as the first Renaissance pope. A person who possessed political savvy and skilled at diplomacy, Nicholas quickly brought about peace in Rome and the surrounding Papal States. He also persuaded Felix V to abdicate, after which he made Felix a cardinal-bishop and a papal legate, and brought about the dissolution of the Council of Basel. After these political successes, he proclaimed 1450 a Jubilee year, which was overshadowed by an outbreak of the plague. He had a very large personal library, which became the basis of the Vatican Library upon his death, and he sponsored beautification and renovation projects throughout the Vatican, employing illustrious artists including Fra Angelico. Frederick III was crowned emperor by Nicholas on March 19, 1452, in St. Peter's. The next year, Europe was rocked by the news that Constantinople had fallen to the Turks. Nicholas died on March 24, 1455, and was surely one of the more moral Renaissance popes.

Callixtus III, the first Spanish pope, succeeded Nicholas V on April 8, 1455. Born Alfonso de Borja, Callixtus demonstrated remarkable energy by organizing a crusade to free Constantinople. He had some successes, but the crusade was largely viewed with indifference by European kings and queens. Callixtus made many appointments of Spanish cardinals to the Curia and appointed his two nephews as cardinals, one of whom was Rodrigo Borgia, who later became Pope Alexander VI. Although he declared Joan of Arc innocent, he renewed anti-Jewish legislation and forbade communication between Christians and Jews. To commemorate the Christian defeat over the Turks at Belgrade in July of 1456, he proclaimed that the feast of the Transfiguration should be observed universally on August 6, which happened to be the day he died in 1458.

The Middle of the Renaissance Papacy:
Pius II to Sixtus IV (1458–1484)

Pius II succeeded Callixtus III on August 19, 1458. Born Enea (Aeneas) Silvio Piccolomini, he had been the secretary to antipope Felix V and had written works defending the authoritative weight of an ecumenical council in general, and specifically, the Council of Basel. Inspired by an illness, he repented of his immoral lifestyle—he was the father of several illegitimate children—and became a priest. When he was elected pope, he may have chosen the name Pius on account of "Pious Aeneas."

Like his predecessor, Callixtus III, Pius was concerned with the Turks, who at that time were invading Europe. Pius called for a crusade against the Turks, and also called for a conference, but the Christian rulers were reluctant to give aid. Thinking he could not convince the European rulers to act because of his prior advances of the conciliar movement before he became pope, he changed his position and wrote two bulls rejecting his earlier position and declaring that a pope could not be subject to an ecumenical council. Pius ran into difficulties with European rulers, in particular King Louis XI of France and the king of Bohemia. He called for another crusade in 1463, but this time he said he would personally lead it. In spite of a lack of personal health and support from European leaders, he set sail for Ancona where he found a small number of Crusaders. He died on August 15, 1464. Pius's genuine conversion and his desire to unite Europe in defense of the Turkish invasion threat are commendable.

Paul II, the nephew of Eugene IV, succeeded Pius II on August 30, 1464. Born Pietro Barbo, he was one of the bad popes in history and known for his vanity, shallowness, and love of entertainment. He was elected pope because he had given the impression that he would seek reform, but he alienated his cardinals by declaring that the pre-electoral pact, which included the cardinals' desired agenda for the next papacy, was merely a set of guidelines instead of mandates. Paul played with the idea of adopting the name Formosus II, but was persuaded to choose another name instead. Paul was a playboy who was more interested in organizing carnivals than councils. He disbanded the college of abbreviators—papal draftsman. When the historian Bartolomeo Platina objected, he was imprisoned and tortured. At the same time however, Paul is known for installing the first printing press in Rome and for collecting works of art.

Although Paul wanted to have a crusade against the Turks, he excommunicated the king of Bohemia, the most capable Christian ruler of leading the crusade, since he suspected him of being a Hussite; he called for a crusade against the king instead. Paul II died of a stroke on July 26, 1471, at the age of fifty-four.

Sixtus IV succeeded Paul II on August 25, 1471. Born Francesco della Rovere, Sixtus was a Franciscan who had grown up in poverty. Although he canonized St. Bonaventure and privileged the mendicant orders, unfortunately, he did not live a life of poverty after becoming pope, seemingly abandoning his vow of poverty. Steeped in nepotism, he appointed six of his nephews as cardinals, one of whom later became Pope Julius II. Sixtus was dragged into Italian politics by Pietro Riario and Giuliano della Rovere, who later became Pope Julius II. One of the affairs Sixtus entangled himself into, was the Pazzi Conspiracy of 1478, which was responsible for the murder of Giuliano de 'Medici and the wounding of Lorenzo, his brother—the intent had been to murder him as well. Although it is doubtful that Sixtus sanctioned the assassination, he was at least aware of the plot. This affair led to a war between Sixtus and the city of Florence.

Sixtus also organized crusades in 1472 and 1481. The crusade in 1481 successfully recovered the Italian city of Otranto. His lavish expenditures on the crusades and the bestowal of gifts on his family depleted the papal treasury. In order to replenish funds, Sixtus began to sell indulgences, which was one of the factors contributing to the Protestant Reformation.

Despite his weaknesses, Sixtus was known for making Rome into a Renaissance city by widening its roads and building new churches. He also founded the Sistine Choir and increased the size of the Vatican Library, which he opened up to scholars. Sixtus died on August 12, 1484.

Although the pontificates of Paul II and Sixtus IV were of a poor quality by moral standards—even as the Renaissance culture was flourishing in Rome, the humanities enjoyed supremacy—the worst was yet to come. With the pontificates of Innocent VIII and Alexander VI, the papacy would achieve an all-time low.

The Beginning of the Protestant Reformation: Innocent VIII to Leo X (1484–1521)

Innocent VIII succeeded Sixtus IV on August 29, 1484. Born Giovanni Battista Cibò, he had the support of Giuliano della Rovere (Julius II) since Cardinal della Rovere thought that he would be able to control him. Inheriting enormous debt, Innocent created and auctioned off church offices.

Although Innocent was initially interested in organizing a crusade against the Turks, he actually ended up working out a deal with Bayezid II, the Ottoman sultan. They agreed that Innocent would keep Bayezid's brother, and potential rival, confined in Rome in exchange for the equivalent of nearly two million dollars in today's currency per year, along with the lance that is said to have pierced the side of Christ.

Innocent empowered the Inquisition in Germany to forcefully punish accusations of witchcraft. Along with his entire court, he was ecstatic when he heard the news that King Ferdinand and Queen Isabella had expelled the Moors from Granada, for which the pope bestowed on them the title "Catholic Kings." Closer to home, Rome was in a state of anarchy on account of the inept rule of Innocent, who died on July 25, 1492.

Alexander VI, the nephew of Callixtus III, succeeded Innocent VIII on August 26, 1492. Born Rodrigo de Borja y Borja,

Alexander's vices are infamous. He had children both before and after his election to the papacy. His life was so scandalous when he had been a cardinal that he had been rebuked by Pius II. Alexander had hoped to become pope in the conclave that elected Sixtus IV, but could not engineer it; the next time around however, he had been able to buy off most of the cardinals. Alexander's administrative skills enabled him to bring order to the papacy where Innocent had brought chaos. In 1497, after his son, Juan, was murdered, Alexander dedicated himself to reforming the church, but his intentions were short lived. He wrote a draft of proposals that was never published and soon returned to his old lifestyle. Cesare, one of Alexander's other sons, aspired to seize large swathes of Europe through intrigue and bribery. He had intended to raise money through assassinations by seizing the victim's property, and simony—bribing potential cardinals. The pope began his long quarrel with Girolamo Savonarola in 1495, which began benignly, but ended with the friar's execution after he had been excommunicated and tortured. Alexander celebrated the Jubilee year 1500 with great pomp. Both Alexander and Cesare fell ill in August 1503, and while some attributed it to malaria, others claimed they had accidentally eaten poisoned food intended for a cardinal. Alexander VI died on August 18, 1503, although Cesare survived the incident, only to die four years later at the age of thirty-one after a group of knights ambushed him.

Pius III, the nephew of Pius II, succeeded Alexander VI on October 1, 1503. Born Francesco Todeschini-Piccolomini, his health was deteriorating when he was elected. He was one of the only popes whom Alexander VI could not bribe to elect him pope, and was also the only cardinal to object to Alexander's handing over large amounts of land to his son, Juan. The newly elected pontiff died on October 18, 1503.

Julius II, the nephew of Sixtus IV, succeeded Pius III on November 1, 1503. Born Giuliano della Rovere, he was a politically astute individual who had been accustomed to being involved in political intrigue. He had to flee Rome during the pontificate of Alexander VI, since he feared that he might be assassinated if he stayed. In France, he could not persuade the king to call a council to depose the pope for simony, so he had to wait until Alexander's reign was over before he could return to Rome in 1503. Giuliano was able to bribe his way to the papacy through promises of money and ecclesiastical benefits. Despite being almost sixty when he was elected pope, he led military expeditions in full armor throughout the Papal States and enlarged them. Although he wasn't too interested in ecclesiastical issues, he gave a dispensation to Henry VIII—which allowed him to take Catherine of Aragon in marriage—established dioceses in South America, called for an ecumenical council—Lateran V— and ironically declared that papal elections in which simony was used to obtain the papacy were null. Julius was a great patron of the arts, commissioning Michelangelo, Raphael, Bramante and others to beautify Rome. The new St. Peter's was commissioned by Julius, but when he used the sale of indulgences to finance the project, he was severely criticized by Protestant Reformers. The papacy of Julius, who died on February 21, 1513, of a fever, is assessed differently by historians. Some hailed him as a forerunner of Italy's unification, while others pointed out that—as a pope wielding a sword with full armor, fathering three illegitimate daughters in his court, and paying for his art work through simony—he was not what a pope should be.

Leo X succeeded Julius II on March 17, 1513. Born Giovanni de' Medici, he was tonsured when he was only seven years old and became a cardinal when he was thirteen. Steeped in theology and the humanities, he was elected pope at the age of thirty-seven without the help of simony, and could have potentially reigned for decades had he not died of malaria only eight years later. His primary goal throughout his pontificate had been to protect his home city of Florence and Italy from invaders. Leo continued Julius's practice of selling indulgences and he also sold cardinal hats to pay for his enormous debts. Martin Luther posted his Ninety-five Theses on the door of the church in Wittenberg, Germany in January 1517 in response to the preaching of indulgences by John Tetzel, a Dominican friar. Leo and his court were completely ignorant of the implications of Luther's revolutionary theses and the power his movement would carry with the princes throughout Germany and the rest of Europe, since they were so engrossed in the financial and political affairs of Italy. Leo X died of malaria on December 1, 1521, leaving the papal treasury hollow and Europe on the brink of a religious conflict, the magnitude of which it had never experienced before.

Conclusion:

Recapitulation and a Look Ahead

The papacy underwent dramatic changes between 904 and 1521. Like book ends, the age called *saeculum obscurum* or "pornocracy" and the Renaissance papacy, two of the most notorious periods of the history of the papacy, enclose this middle era of the history of the popes.

Sergius III and his entanglement with the Theophylact family led to the papacy being wrapped around the fingers of two powerful women and their progeny. With the decline of the Theophylact family, came the rise of the Tusculan family, an extension of the Theophylact family. Other powerful families flexed their muscles as well, including the Crescentii, Orsini, Borgia, and de' Medici families. The nepotistic genealogy of the popes attests to the high level of corruption the papacy was involved in, which culminated in the pontificate of Alexander VI, who was arguably the most corrupt pope in history. In many cases, the popes of this era allowed their familial interests to take precedence over the spiritual interests of the church, but throughout all of the vicissitudes of history and the scandals of the papacy, the papacy endured.

In the beginning of the High Middle Ages, the papacy was transformed by St. Gregory VII, who ensured that the papacy would exercise a tremendous amount of power in the Middle

Ages and beyond. Gregory, a canon lawyer, sought a legal basis for the Church's power, in particular for the power of the papacy. He staunchly defended the Church's right in regard to the Investiture Controversy against Henry IV, by placing his realm in a state of interdict and informing his subjects that they were freed from owing an allegiance to him. This was a wake-up call to the other leaders as to how much power a pope could wield in a thoroughly Christian Europe.

In 1096, the First Crusade, one of many Christian military expeditions intended to free the Holy Land from Muslim domination, was launched in response to the call from Bl. Urban II to take up arms. Although the intention of many of the popes and crusaders was noble, some of the acts of the crusaders were completely deplorable, such as the sack of Constantinople in 1204. Despite its failures, the crusades gave Europe and the Church a foothold against the threat of militant Islam, and created a homeostasis in which both Muslims and Christians exercised dominance in their particular geographical regions and spheres.

Frederick Barbarossa's locking of horns with the popes set an example to other European leaders, showing them that they, too, could push the envelope and that the papacy was not all-powerful. The situation in Rome eventually declined to such an extent, that the popes had to move out of Rome in the early fourteenth century, thus inaugurating the Avignon Papacy, commonly known as the Babylonian Captivity of the Papacy. As soon as the papacy was out of the frying pan, it went into the oven with the unstable papacy of Urban VI which resulted in the Great Western Schism. The peace that ensued with the end of the schism led to the Renaissance Papacy, which had permitted the popes to contract great artists and to transform Rome into an opulent Renaissance city, but since the debt that such projects accrued were financed by the selling of indulgences, the stage had been set for the eruption of the Protestant Reformation. The corruption of the popes, the Curia, and the other church leaders was finally catching up to them, and the princes of Europe would take advantage of the religious fervor of the Reformers to grab their pieces of the pie from the hands of the Catholic Church.

Just like the early Church, the Catholic Church emerged out of the crisis of the Protestant Reformation stronger than it was before, not necessarily in terms of its temporal power, but most certainly in terms of its moral fiber. The Counter-Reformation effectively reformed the Catholic Church, although exactly how effective this reform was, has been debated. Nevertheless, one of the darkest eras of the Catholic Church was finally coming to an end with the rise of Protestantism, which was a clarion call to the leaders of the Catholic Church to awaken from their spiritual slumber.

Three of the major factors that contributed to the demarcation between the Renaissance period and the modern era were the invention of the printing press, the voyage of Christopher Columbus, and the scientific revolution. When Johannes Gutenberg invented the printing press circa 1439, it had remarkable ramifications for Western society. It increased literacy throughout Europe, bolstered academics with the proliferation of books, and was used as a tool of propaganda for religious and political purposes alike. With the expedition of Christopher Columbus to the Americas in 1492, the New World was opened to Europe. Missionaries poured into the Americas and were greatly aided by the Counter Reformation movement. About thirty years after the death of Leo X, the scientific revolution was underway in Europe with the discoveries of Nicholas Copernicus, a Catholic priest. About fifty years after that, the programmatic writings of Sir Francis Bacon paved the way for scientific experimentation. The scientific revolution quickly and radically changed humanity's understanding of philosophy, technology, and the world.For all of these reasons, there is a stark difference between fourteenth-century and sixteenth-century Europe. The papacy's agenda followed suite by using the printing press, turning its eyes toward the Americas, and founding the Observatory of the Roman College in 1774. The Holy See's response to these three events—i.e. the invention of the printing press, the voyage of Columbus, and the scientific revolution—propelled the papacy into the modern era.

Suggestions for Further Reading

Balthasar, Hans Urs von. *The Office of Peter and the Structure of the Church.* 2nd edition. Translated by Andrée Emery. San Francisco: Ignatius, 1986.

Duffy, Eamon. *Saints & Sinners: A History of the Popes.* New Haven, Conn.: Yale University Press, 1997.

Kelly, J.N.D. *The Oxford Dictionary of Popes.* New York: Oxford University Press, 1986.

McBrien, Richard P. *Lives of the Popes: The Pontiffs from St. Peter to John Paul II.* San Francisco: HarperSanFrancisco, 1997.

Ratzinger, Joseph Cardinal. *Called to Communion: Understanding the Church Today.* Translated by Adrian Walker. San Francisco: Ignatius, 1996.

Please enjoy the first two chapters of Pope Francis: Pastor of Mercy, written by Michael J. Ruszala, as available from Wyatt North Publishing.

Pope Francis: Pastor of Mercy

Chapter 1

There is something about Pope Francis that captivates and delights people, even people who hardly know anything about him. He was elected in only two days of the conclave, yet many who tried their hand at speculating on who the next pope might be barely included him on their lists. The evening of Wednesday, March 13, 2013, the traditional white smoke poured out from the chimney of the Sistine Chapel and spread throughout the world by way of television, Internet, radio, and social media, signaling the beginning of a new papacy.

As the light of day waned from the Eternal City, some 150,000 people gathered watching intently for any movement behind the curtained door to the loggia of St. Peter's. A little after 8:00 p.m., the doors swung open and Cardinal Tauran emerged to pronounce the traditional and joyous Latin formula to introduce the new Bishop of Rome: "Annuncio vobis gaudium magnum; habemus papam!" ("I announce to you a great joy: we have a pope!") He then announced the new Holy Father's identity: "Cardinalem Bergoglio..."

The name Bergoglio, stirred up confusion among most of the faithful who flooded the square that were even more clueless than the television announcers were, who scrambled to figure out who exactly the new pope was. Pausing briefly, Cardinal

Tauran continued by announcing the name of the new pope: "...qui sibi nomen imposuit Franciscum" ("who takes for himself the name Francis"). Whoever this man may be, his name choice resonated with all, and the crowd erupted with jubilant cheers. A few moments passed before the television announcers and their support teams informed their global audiences that the man who was about to walk onto the loggia dressed in white was Cardinal Jorge Mario Bergoglio, age 76, of Buenos Aires, Argentina.

To add to the bewilderment and kindling curiosity, when the new pope stepped out to the thunderous applause of the crowd in St. Peter's Square, he did not give the expected papal gesture of outstretched arms. Instead, he gave only a simple and modest wave. Also, before giving his first apostolic blessing, he bowed asking the faithful, from the least to the greatest, to silently pray for him. These acts were only the beginning of many more words and gestures, such as taking a seat on the bus with the cardinals, refusing a popemobile with bulletproof glass, and paying his own hotel bill after his election, that would raise eyebrows among some familiar with papal customs and delight the masses.

Is he making a pointed critique of previous pontificates? Is he simply posturing a persona to the world at large to make a point? The study of the life of Jorge Mario Bergoglio gives a clear answer, and the answer is no. This is simply who he is as a man and as a priest. The example of his thought- provoking gestures flows from his character, his life experiences, his religious vocation, and his spirituality. This book uncovers the life of the 266th Bishop of Rome, Jorge Mario Bergoglio, also known as Father Jorge, a name he preferred even while he was an archbishop and cardinal.

What exactly do people find so attractive about Pope Francis? Aldo Cagnoli, a layman who developed a friendship with the Pope when he was serving as a cardinal, shares the following: "The greatness of the man, in my humble opinion lies not in building walls or seeking refuge behind his wisdom and office, but rather in dealing with everyone judiciously, respectfully, and with humility, being willing to learn at any moment of life; that is what Father Bergoglio means to me" (as quoted in Ch. 12 of Pope Francis: Conversations with Jorge Bergoglio, previously published as El Jesuita [The Jesuit]).

At World Youth Day 2013, in Rio de Janeiro, Brazil, three million young people came out to celebrate their faith with

Pope Francis. Doug Barry, from EWTN's Life on the Rock, interviewed youth at the event on what features stood out to them about Pope Francis. The young people seemed most touched by his authenticity. One young woman from St. Louis said, "He really knows his audience. He doesn't just say things to say things... And he is really sincere and genuine in all that he does." A friend agreed: "He was looking out into the crowd and it felt like he was looking at each one of us...." A young man from Canada weighed in: "You can actually relate to [him]... for example, last night he was talking about the World Cup and athletes." A young woman added, "I feel he means what he says... he practices what he preaches... he states that he's there for the poor and he actually means it."

The Holy Spirit guided the College of Cardinals in its election of Pope Francis to meet the needs of the Church following the historic resignation of Pope Benedict XVI due to old age. Representing the growth and demographic shift in the Church throughout the world and especially in the Southern Hemisphere, Pope Francis is the first non-European pope in almost 1,300 years. He is also the first Jesuit pope. Pope Francis comes with a different background and set of experiences. Both as archbishop and as pope, his flock knows him for his humility, ascetic frugality in solidarity with the poor, and closeness. He was born in Buenos Aires to a family of Italian immigrants, earned a diploma in chemistry, and followed a priestly vocation in the Jesuit order after an experience of God's mercy while receiving the sacrament of Reconciliation. Even though he is known for his smile and humor, the world also recognizes Pope Francis as a stern figure that stands against the evils of the world and challenges powerful government officials, when necessary.

The Church he leads is one that has been burdened in the West by the aftermath of sex abuse scandals and increased secularism. It is also a Church that is experiencing shifting in numbers out of the West and is being challenged with religious persecution in the Middle East, Asia, and Africa. The Vatican that Pope Francis has inherited is plagued by cronyism and scandal. This Holy Father knows, however, that his job is not merely about numbers, politics, or even success. He steers clear of pessimism knowing that he is the head of Christ's Body on earth and works with Christ's grace. This is the man God has chosen in these times to lead his flock.

Chapter 2: Early Life in Argentina

Jorge Mario Bergoglio was born on December 17, 1936, in the Flores district of Buenos Aires. The district was a countryside locale outside the main city during the nineteenth century and many rich people in its early days called this place home. By the time Jorge was born, Flores was incorporated into the city of Buenos Aires and became a middle class neighborhood. Flores is also the home of the beautiful Romantic-styled Basilica of San José de Flores, built in 1831, with its dome over the altar, spire over the entrance, and columns at its facade. It was the Bergoglios' parish church and had much significance in Jorge's life.

Jorge's father's family had arrived in Argentina in 1929, immigrating from Piedimonte in northern Italy. They were not the only ones immigrating to the country. In the late nineteenth century, Argentina became industrialized and the government promoted immigration from Europe. During that time, the land prospered and Buenos Aires earned the moniker "Paris of the South." In the late nineteenth and early twentieth centuries waves of immigrants from Italy, Spain, and other European countries came off ships in the port of Buenos Aires. Three of Jorge's great uncles were the first in the family to immigrate to Argentina in 1922 searching for better employment opportunities after World War I. They established a paving company in Buenos Aires and built a four-story building for their company with the city's first elevator. Jorge's father and paternal grandparents followed the brothers in order to keep the family together and to escape Mussolini's fascist regime in Italy. Jorge's father and grandfather also helped with the business for a time. His father, Mario, who had been an accountant for a rail company in Italy, provided similar services for the family business (Cardinal Bergoglio recalls more on the story of his family's immigration and his early life in Ch. 1 of Conversations with Jorge Bergoglio).

Providentially, the Bergoglios were long delayed in liquidating their assets in Italy; this forced them to miss the ship they planned to sail on, the doomed Pricipessa Mafalda, which sank off the northern coast of Brazil before reaching Buenos Aires. The family took the Giulio Cesare instead and arrived safely in Argentina with Jorge's Grandma Rosa. Grandma Rosa wore a fur coat stuffed with the money the family brought with them from Italy. Economic hard times eventually hit Argentina in 1932 and the family's paving business went under, but the Bergoglio brothers began anew.

Jorge's father, Mario, met his mother Regina at Mass in 1934. Regina was born in Argentina, but her parents were also Italian immigrants. Mario and Regina married the following year after meeting. Jorge, the eldest of their five children, was born in 1936. Jorge fondly recalls his mother gathering the children around the radio on Sunday afternoons to listen to opera and explain the story. A true porteño, as the inhabitants of the port city of Buenos Aires are called, Jorge liked to play soccer, listen to Latin music, and dance the tango. Jorge's paternal grandparents lived around the corner from his home. He greatly admired his Grandma Rosa, and keeps her written prayer for her grandchildren with him until this day. Jorge recalls that while his grandparents kept their personal conversations in Piedmontese, Mario chose mostly to speak Spanish, preferring to look forward rather than back. Still, Jorge grew up speaking both Italian and Spanish.

Upon entering secondary school at the age of thirteen, his father insisted that Jorge begin work even though the family, in their modest lifestyle, was not particularly in need of extra income. Mario Bergoglio wanted to teach the boy the value of work and found several jobs for him during his adolescent years. Jorge worked in a hosiery factory for several years as a cleaner and at a desk. When he entered technical school to study food chemistry, Jorge found a job working in a laboratory. He worked under a woman who always challenged him to do his work thoroughly. He remembers her, though, with both fondness and sorrow. Years later, she was kidnapped and murdered along with members of her family because of her political views during the Dirty War, a conflict in the 1970's and 80's between the military dictatorship and guerrilla fighters in which thousands of Argentineans disappeared.

Initially unhappy with his father's decision to make him work, Jorge recalls later in his life that work was a valuable formative experience for him that taught him responsibility, realism, and how the world operated. He learned that a person's self worth often comes from their work, which led him to become committed later in life to promote a just culture of work rather than simply encouraging charity or entitlement. He believes that people need meaningful work in order to thrive. During his boyhood through his priestly ministry, he experienced the gulf in Argentina between the poor and the well off, which left the poor having few opportunities for gainful employment.

At the age of twenty-one, Jorge became dangerously ill. He was diagnosed with severe pneumonia and cysts. Part of his upper right lung was removed, and each day Jorge endured the pain and discomfort of saline fluid pumped through his chest to clear his system. Jorge remembers that the only person that was able to comfort him during this time was a religious sister who had catechized him from childhood, Sister Dolores. She exposed him to the true meaning of suffering with this simple statement: "You are imitating Christ." This stuck with him, and his sufferings during that time served as a crucible for his character, teaching him how to distinguish what is important in life from what is not. He was being prepared for what God was calling him to do in life, his vocation.

Printed in Great Britain
by Amazon

78835663R00081